New York

THE BIG APPLE
QUOTE BOOK

EDITED BY BOB BLAISDELL

DOVER PUBLICATIONS, INC.
MINEOLA, NEW YORK

Bibliographical Note

New York: The Big Apple Quote Book is a new work, first published by Dover Publications, Inc., in 2011.

Library of Congress Cataloging-in-Publication Data

New York : the Big Apple quote book / edited by Bob Blaisdell.
       p. cm.
  Includes bibliographical references.
  ISBN-13: 978-0-486-47866-1
  ISBN-10: 0-486-47866-1
    1. New York (N.Y.)—Quotations, maxims, etc. 2. Quotations, English. 3. Quotations. I. Blaisdell, Robert.

PN6084.N38N48 2011
974.7'1—dc22

                                    2011010619

Manufactured in the United States by Courier Corporation
47866101
www.doverpublications.com

Contents

INTRODUCTION

Even before moving to New York City, I was dreaming about New York, reading about New York. Joseph Mitchell's *The Bottom of the Harbor* was a particular favorite. From rivermen to rat-catchers, everyone had a big personality; everyone was interesting and knowledgeable. Yes, Mitchell may be about the best *New Yorker* writer ever, but he really *saw* something, he *caught* something: "The rats of New York are quicker-witted than those on farms, and they can outthink any man who has not made a study of their habits." The people (and animals!) Mitchell profiled had a tough and ready character I envied and admired. As a new New Yorker, I devoured first-hand accounts about the Big Apple experience, especially about the subway, which for me represented the glory of New York. As Lawrence Block says, "Writers who don't take the subway? They must be out of their minds." To ride the subway was (and still is) to be expectant, alert, and excited.

For this collection, I gave myself up to the pleasures of quoting from fine and famous and handy books and articles; I selected those sentiments that seemed striking, witty and, if not true, then at least absolutely, ruthlessly *sincere*. *That quote*—I would think—*that* characterizes New York: "It is one of the oldest places in the United States, but doesn't live in retrospect like the professionally picturesque provinces," observed the great A. J. Liebling. "Any city may have one period of magnificence, like Boston or New Orleans or San

Francisco, but it takes a real one to keep renewing itself until the past is perennially forgotten." And then what about *this* one, in the paper just the other day: "There are 1,289 pages in *The Encyclopedia of New York City,* and not a single entry is devoted to toll plazas. They set the gruff, egalitarian tone of the city: Everyone waits, everyone pays" (excellent, Mr. Manny Fernandez!). A visiting missionary, way back in 1679, had an experience that is so marvelous it's unimaginable: "In passing through this island we sometimes encountered such a sweet smell in the air that we stood still." *Unimaginable?* Imagine this: nowadays, I occasionally catch myself coming to a standstill on the busy sidewalks of Manhattan, captivated by "such a sweet smell" that only after a moment do I realize it emanates from one of those sidewalk carts peddling copper-pot honey-roasted nuts.

As for my unfortunate misquotations, misattributions, and typographical errors, I blush and apologize. Write and correct me, please. A fabulous quote that somebody else collected I usually reference simply to the quote-finder and not to the original source, and I often, but could not always, note the year the statement was made. As for the arrangement of the quotations within the sections, they are usually loosely chronological, with occasional reordering for emphasis, thematic unity, or contrast.

I am not done looking for quotes. There are so many good books about New York and New Yorkers and New York-ness that I haven't yet read, that I hope in the afterlife there are libraries (and subway trains on which I can ride while I read). So I thank the librarians at the New York Public Library and Columbia's Butler Library for providing me with books and sources; and I also thank, historically speaking, John Manbeck, my mentor in all things Brooklyn. For the writers and speakers and quotation-compilers whose sparkling words I have quoted, I offer the deepest appreciation for their illuminating observations of the Big Apple.

—*Bob Blaisdell*
February 2010

New York

THE BIG APPLE
QUOTE BOOK

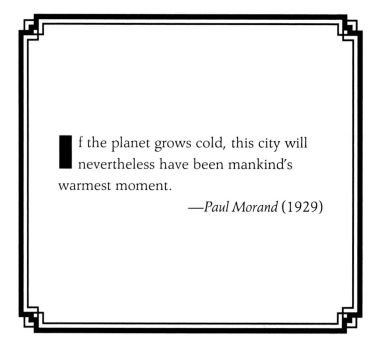

If the planet grows cold, this city will nevertheless have been mankind's warmest moment.

—*Paul Morand* (1929)

1

I Love New York

I love New York. How could I not love a city that contains both Gray's Papaya and the Brooklyn Bridge? But maybe I too have been stuck in this bad marriage too long, hopelessly in love not with the city, the hard economic realities of it, the years of being part of the crowd, but with the skyline, that suggestion in lights that this place is both unreachable and a goal. That it is, in short, poetry. That is the city that pulls me, the city I carry around in my head.

—*Elizabeth Gold*

❖ ❖ ❖

To say that New York came up to its advance billing would be the baldest of understatements. Being there was like being in heaven without going to all the bother and expense of dying.

—*P. G. Wodehouse*

The beautiful city, the city of hurried and sparkling
        waters! the city of spires and masts!
The city nested in bays! my city!
The city of such women, I am mad with them! I will
        return after death to be with them!
The city of such young men, I swear I cannot live
        happy, without I often go talk, walk, eat,
        drink, sleep, with them!

                                      —*Walt Whitman*

❖ ❖ ❖

. . . I was in love with New York. I do not mean "love" in
any colloquial way, I mean that I was in love with the city,
the way you love the first person who ever touches you and
never love anyone quite that way again.

                                      —*Joan Didion*

If Paris is the setting for a romance, New York is
the perfect city in which to get over one, to get over
anything. Here the lost *douceur de vivre* is forgotten and the
intoxication of living takes over.

—*Cyril Connolly*

❖ ❖ ❖

But, ah! Manhattan's sights and sounds, her smells
Her crowds, her throbbing force, the thrill that comes
From being of her a part, her subtle spells, her slums—
Oh God! the stark unutterable pity,
To be dead, and never again behold my city!

—*James Weldon Johnson*

❖ ❖ ❖

. . . the great place of the western continent, the heart,
the brain, the focus, the main spring, the pinnacle, the
extremity, the no more beyond, of the New World.

—*Walt Whitman*

❖

Of course I'll return to New York. It's my home. Is there any place else? I'd rather be a lamppost on Seventh Avenue than a queen in another country.

—*Grace Watson* (1971)

❖ ❖ ❖

Commuters give the city its tidal restlessness, natives give it solidity and continuity, but the settlers give it passion.

—*E. B. White* (1949)

❖ ❖ ❖

New York cannot help but stand as a special order: the place which is not wilderness, the place of light and warmth and the envelopment of the human swarm, the place in which everyone is awake and laughing at three in the morning.

—*Vincent McHugh* (1938)

❖ ❖ ❖

Someone from out of town I met last night asked me why I live in New York. I told him I live here because of the tempo and the fast track, because there are always so many more choices. I live here because it ruins you for any other place.

—*Jean Bach* (2006)

I don't have no intentions of leaving the city. Not yet, anyways. I went back to the reservation a couple of times and I could only stay a week. There's nothing to do out there. This is where the action is. For the time being, I like Manhattan.

—*Wilford "Chief" Parriette* (1999)

❖ ❖ ❖

New York took me over. New York has become my natural habitat. I'd be fenced in anywhere else. I can behave exactly as I want: I can appear, I can disappear.

—*Lola Szladits* (2006)

❖ ❖ ❖

The thing I've found is the people that are most enthusiastic about living in New York are often people like me who are originally from somewhere else.

—*Kenneth Jackson* (1995)

New York is an ugly city, a dirty city. Its climate is a scandal, its politics are used to frighten children, its traffic is madness, its competition is murderous. But there is one thing about it—once you have lived in New York and it has become your home, no place else is good enough.

—*John Steinbeck* (1943)

❖ ❖ ❖

There are roughly three New Yorks. There is, first, the New York of the man or woman who was born here, who takes the city for granted and accepts its size and its turbulence as natural and inevitable. Second, there is the New York of the commuter—the city that is devoured by locusts each day and spat out each night. Third, there is the New York of the person who was born somewhere else and came to New York in quest of something.

—*E. B. White* (1949)

❖ ❖ ❖

When I came to New York people immediately accepted me in the sense that I was anonymous. And I liked that.

—*Patti Smith*

---❖---

A person who had really been to New York was more wonderful to me than angels.

—*Langston Hughes*

❖ ❖ ❖

I like New York in June, how about you? It is, of course, still May but I like New York in May too. In fact I like New York period. It is stimulating and busy and the apartment is charming.

—*Noel Coward* (1957)

❖ ❖ ❖

More and more too, the *old name* absorbs into me— MANAHATTA, the "place encircled by many swift tides and sparkling waters." How fit a name for America's great democratic island city!

—*Walt Whitman* (1879)

Every true New Yorker believes with all his heart that when a New Yorker is tired of New York, he is tired of life.

—*Robert Moses*

❖ ❖ ❖

Any real New Yorker is a you-name-it-we-have-it snob . . . whose heart brims with sympathy for the millions of unfortunates who through misfortune, misguidedness or pure stupidity live anywhere else in the world.

—*Russell Lynes* (1965)

❖ ❖ ❖

My favorite city in the world is New York. Sure it's dirty—but like a beautiful lady smoking a cigar.

—*Joan Rivers*

❖ ❖ ❖

I've always loved New York. It just never loved me back.

—*James Edwards, a homeless man*

A week after I moved to Manhattan in the sultry summer of 1985, I stepped out my front door one morning and was struck by a dizzy joy, a lightning conviction that I belonged here, that I should have been born here, that being born in Toronto had been a terrible mistake.

—*Michele Landsberg* (1989)

❖ ❖ ❖

A good city street neighborhood achieves a marvel of balance between its people's determination to have essential privacy and their simultaneous wishes for differing degrees of contact, enjoyment or help from the people around.

—*Jane Jacobs* (1961)

❖ ❖ ❖

It rained earlier in the day and now, at one in the afternoon, for a minute and a half, New York is washed clean. The streets glitter in the pale spring sunlight. Cars radiate dust-free happiness. Storefront windows sparkle mindlessly. Even people look made anew.

—*Vivian Gornick* (1987)

I love Chinatown. I love the outdoor market that has grown up along Canal Street, and I love the food stores where I can't ever seem to get anyone to tell me what anything is in English.

—*Calvin Trillin*

❖ ❖ ❖

Assertive people are not tolerated in California. My friends there would tell me one of two things. They either said: "Go into therapy" or "Go to New York." And so I actually did kind of both of those things.

—*Bill Heidbreder, quoted by Howard Kaplan* (2005)

❖ ❖ ❖

I was in love with Harlem long before I got there. Had I been a rich young man, I would have bought a house in Harlem and built musical steps up to the front door, and installed chimes that at the press of a button played Ellington tunes.

—*Langston Hughes* (1963)

Whenever I see New York at night a terrific surge of love comes over me. New York is hope and challenge; good and evil; mystery and change and, most of all, the unexpected.

—*Alex Phillips*

❖ ❖ ❖

The most positive thing of all is that nobody ever has to be alone in New York. You're alone with New York, which makes a whole world of difference. What other companionship could be so varied, stimulating, dramatic, and so available?

—*Anita Loos and Helen Hayes* (1972)

❖ ❖ ❖

You can do what you want in New York. You can start a business and people will let you live. In a small town, if they don't like you they'll figure a way to keep you out. In New York, you take people one by one.

—*Bradley Cunningham* (2006)

Everyone at one time or another tries to explain to himself why he likes New York better than any place else. A man who worked for me liked it because if he couldn't sleep he could go to an all-night movie. That's as good a reason as any.

—*John Steinbeck* (1943)

❖ ❖ ❖

The finest thing about New York City, I think, is that it is like one of those complicated Renaissance clocks where on one level an allegorical marionette pops out to mark the day of the week, on another a skeleton death bangs the quarter hour with his scythe, and on a third the Twelve Apostles do a cakewalk.

—*A. J. Liebling* (1938)

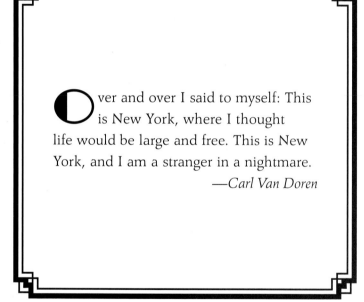

Over and over I said to myself: This is New York, where I thought life would be large and free. This is New York, and I am a stranger in a nightmare.

—*Carl Van Doren*

I Hate New York

❖

New York is notoriously the largest and least loved of any of our great cities. Why should it be loved as a city? It is never the same city for [a] dozen years altogether. A man born in New York forty years ago finds nothing, absolutely nothing, of the New York he knew.

—*Harper's Magazine* (1856)

❖ ❖ ❖

Speaking of New York as a traveler, I have two faults to find with it. In the first place, there is nothing to see; in the second place, there is no mode of getting about to see anything.

—*Anthony Trollope* (1862)

❖ ❖ ❖

The only trouble about this town is that it is too large. You cannot accomplish anything in the way of business, you cannot even pay a friendly call, without devoting a whole day to it.

—*Mark Twain* (1867)

❖

People talk of the pride a New Yorker must feel in this great city! To be a citizen of New York is a disgrace. A domicile on Manhattan Island is a thing to be confessed with apologies and humiliation.

—*George Templeton Strong* (1868)

❖ ❖ ❖

The very sign of its energy is that it doesn't believe in itself; it fails to succeed, even at the cost of millions, in persuading you that it does. Its mission would appear to be, exactly, to gild the temporary with its gold.

—*Henry James* (1907)

❖ ❖ ❖

New York is something awful, something monstrous. I like to walk the streets, lost, but I recognize that New York is the world's great lie. New York is Senegal with machines. The only things that the United States has given to the world are skyscrapers, jazz, and cocktails. Besides black art, there is only automation and mechanization.

—*Federico Garcia Lorca* (c. 1929)

This man-trap of gigantic dimensions, devouring manhood, denies in its affected riot of personality any individuality whatsoever.

—*Frank Lloyd Wright*

❖ ❖ ❖

The plain fact of the matter is that New York is too good for New Yorkers. Complete appreciation will come only when some Vesuvius has laid it low and posterity is forced to dig down into the dust to bring to light the buried treasure.

—*Heywood Broun*

❖ ❖ ❖

There are some who say with passion that the only real advantage of living in New York is that all its residents ascend to heaven directly after their deaths, having served their full term in purgatory right on Manhattan Island.

—*Alexander Klein*

❖

No one as yet has approached the management of New York in a proper spirit; that is to say, regarding it as the shiftless outcome of squalid barbarism and reckless extravagance.

—*Rudyard Kipling*

❖ ❖ ❖

New York looks as ever: stiff, machine-made, and against nature. It is so mechanical there is not the sense of death.

—*D. H. Lawrence* (1924)

❖ ❖ ❖

"Brother Hall," I said to myself, "which city is the most wicked city, pluperfect and parboiled, you've ever been in?" Without a bit of hesitation the answer came forth, "New York, N. Y." Consequently, I got on a train and came here and took root.

—*Reverend James Jefferson Davis Hall,*
quoted by Joseph Mitchell (1943)

❖

It is a world completely rotten with wealth, power,
senility, indifference, Puritanism and mental hygiene,
poverty and waste, technological futility and aimless
violence, and yet I cannot help but feel it has about it
something of the dawning of the universe.

—*Jean Baudrillard* (1988)

❖ ❖ ❖

New York has more commissioners than Des Moines,
Iowa, has residents, including the Commissioner
for Making Sure the Sidewalks Are Always Blocked
By Steaming Fetid Mounds of Garbage the Size of
Appalachian Foothills.

—*Dave Barry*

❖ ❖ ❖

I loathe the suspicion New York arouses in me vis-à-vis
other human beings.

—*Magda Salvesen* (2006)

"Me and New York," she has said. "We were like partners
in a bad marriage.
We loved each other . . . at least I loved it . . . but we
couldn't live together."
I know what she means. She speaks for all those who
ever arrived in this city dreaming romantic dreams of what
they imagine will be the actor's or artist's life or just life,
only to wake up years later in a lonely room surrounded
by empty boxes of Chinese takeout.

—*Elizabeth Gold* (2005)

❖ ❖ ❖

I tried to look at all the renovation in my neighborhood
as a gladsom indicator of prosperity, but it didn't help . . .
I don't want to live in this city any more, where the very
walls perish around you only to be reborn in the agony of
time. I want to live in a city that's done.

—*Said Shirazi* (2001)

There is no thrill in the world like entering, for the first time, New York harbor,—coming in from the flat monotony of the sea to this rise of dreams and beauty. New York is truly the dream city,—city of the towers near God, city of hopes and visions, of spires seeking in the windy air loveliness and perfection.

—*Langston Hughes* (1925)

3

It's a Nice Place to Visit

❖

Whatever any other city has, New York has more of; be it gay or sad, good or criminal, plain or fancy.

—*Warren Moscow* (1967)

❖ ❖ ❖

I think New York one of the finest cities I ever saw, and as much superior to every other in the Union (Philadelphia not excepted), as London to Liverpool, or Paris to Rouen.

—*Frances Trollope* (1831)

❖ ❖ ❖

Whoever visits New York feels as he does in a watchmaker's shop; everybody goes there for the true time, and feels on leaving it as if he had been wound up or regulated anew.

—*Thomas Dwight* (1833)

❖ ❖ ❖

A bulger of a place it is. The number of ships beat me all hollow, and looked for all the world like a big clearing in the West, with the dead trees all standing.

—*Davy Crockett* (1835)

❖

The first impression of a stranger entering New York is that it was built the night before.

—*New York Daily News* (1860)

❖ ❖ ❖

Nobody is quiet here, no more am I. The rush and restlessness pleases me, and I like, for a little, the dash of the stream. I am not received as a god, which I like, too.

—*William Makepeace Thackeray*

❖ ❖ ❖

For Europeans New York is America, but for Americans it is the beginning of Europe.

—*Paul de Rousiers* (1890)

❖ ❖ ❖

As I drew near New York I was first amused, and then somewhat staggered, by the cautious and grisly tales that went around. You would have thought we were to land upon a cannibal island. You must speak to no one in the streets, as they would not leave 'til you were rooked and beaten.

—*Robert Louis Stevenson* (1905)

Here I was in New York, city of prose and fantasy, of capitalist automation, its streets a triumph of cubism, its moral philosophy that of the dollar. New York impressed me tremendously because, more than any other city in the world, it is the fullest expression of our modern age.

—*Leon Trotsky* (1917)

❖ ❖ ❖

The visiting Englishman, or the visiting Californian, is convinced that New York is made up of millions of gay pixies, flitting about constantly in a sophisticated manner in search of a new thrill.

—*Robert Benchley*

❖ ❖ ❖

There is no thrill in the world like entering, for the first time, New York harbor, . . . New York is truly the dream city, —city of the towers near God, city of hopes and visions, of spires seeking in the windy air loveliness and perfection.

—*Langston Hughes* (1925)

A New Yorker doesn't have to discover New York. He knows it's there all the time.

—Whitey Blimstein, quoted by A. J. Liebling (1938)

❖ ❖ ❖

The bus passenger coming down over the Boston Post Road from New England watches traffic slow and thicken as the environs' towns become larger, draw together, give off the effect of a brisker life. There is a moment in which he asks himself: "Are we in the city yet? Is this New York?"

—Vincent McHugh (1938)

❖ ❖ ❖

May I point to one exhibit that I hope all visitors will note, and that is the city of New York itself.

—Mayor Fiorello La Guardia, on the opening day of the World's Fair (1939)

It wasn't until I got to New York that I became Kansan. Everyone there kept reminding me that they were Jewish or Irish, or whatever, so I kept reminding them that I was Midwestern. Before I knew it, I actually began to brag about being from Kansas!

—*William Inge* (1941)

❖ ❖ ❖

To the visiting non-competitive European all is unending delight . . . where every language is spoken and xenophobia almost unknown, where every purse and appetite is catered for.

—*Cyril Connolly* (1947)

❖ ❖ ❖

At Times Square, awash in light, waterfalls and rivers of light, news running around buildings in light, we stared in rapture at a giant woman, her head flung back, a Camel tilted in her fingers, giant rings of smoke puffing from her mouth more miraculously than water struck from a rock.

—*Michele Landsberg* (c. 1950)

If you are confused ask somebody. New Yorkers are very helpful. However, the first person you ask will give you the wrong answer. So ask loudly enough that others will overhear and make corrections. New Yorkers love to correct each other.

—*George Weller* (1983)

❖ ❖ ❖

New Yorkers are nice about giving you street directions; in fact they seem quite proud of knowing where they are themselves.

—*Katherine Brush* (1969)

❖ ❖ ❖

The metaphor that many first-time visitors have employed is of the steam which rises from manholes at some street corners—part of an underground heating system for older buildings. They see this as a symbol of the city's latent energy.

—*Michael Leapman*

The New York of today is not the New York of fifty years ago; and fifty years hence where will the New York of today be?

—*Henry Philip Tappan* (1855)

4

THAT'S HISTORY

❖

The present in New York is so powerful that the past
is lost.

—*John Jay Chapman* (1909)

❖ ❖ ❖

In the reading room in the New York Public Library
All sorts of souls were bent over in silence reading the past
Or the present, or maybe it was the future
Devoted to silence and the flowering of the imagination.

—*Richard Eberhart* (1939–1986)

❖ ❖ ❖

New York is where the future comes to audition.

—*Ed Koch, mayor of New York* (1978–1989)

❖ ❖ ❖

Any city may have one period of magnificence, like
Boston or New Orleans or San Francisco, but it takes
a real one to keep renewing itself until the past is
perennially forgotten.

—*A. J. Liebling* (1938)

New York, on the surface the most volatile and kaleidoscopic of cities, is in essence, I think, peculiarly permanent. Contrary to the popular view, in fundamentals it really changes very little down the generations.

—*Jan Morris* (1969)

❖ ❖ ❖

This is a very good land to fall with and a pleasant land to see.

—*A mate aboard Henry Hudson's* Half Moon (1609)

❖ ❖ ❖

Had we cows, hogs, and other cattle fit for food (which we daily expect in the first ships) we would not wish to return to Holland, for whatever we desire in the paradise of Holland, is here to be found.

—*Dutch colonist* (c. 1624)

It is somewhat strange that among these most barbarous people, there are few or none cross-eyed, blind, crippled, lame, hunch-backed or limping men; all are well-fashioned people, strong and sound of body, well fed, without blemish.

—*Nicholaes van Wassenaer,*
regarding the native Lenapes (1626)

❖ ❖ ❖

Its location and topography—"like a great natural pier ready to receive the commerce of the world" is how one early writer described it—would make it the gate through which Europeans could reach the unimaginable vastness of the North American land mass.

—*Russell Shorto*

❖ ❖ ❖

They have purchased the Island Manhattes from the Indians for the value of 60 guilders; it is 11,000 morgens in size.

—*Pieter Schaghen, Dutch official and author* (1626)

❖

Whereas the Company is put to great expense both in building fortifications and in supporting soldiers and sailors, we have therefore resolved to demand from the Indians who dwell around here and whom heretofore we have protected against their enemies, some contributions in the form of skins, maize and seawan.

—*Willem Kieft, in-country director of the West India Company, on plans to tax the Native Americans* (c. 1630s)

❖ ❖ ❖

Its capital was a tiny collection of rough buildings perched on the edge of a limitless wilderness, but its muddy lanes and waterfront were prowled by a Babel of peoples . . . It was Manhattan, in other words, right from the start.

—*Russell Shorto* (2005)

The land of itself is fertile, and capable of being entirely cultivated by an abundance of people.

—*Peter Stuyvesant, the director of New Netherland; letter to the directors of the West India Company in Amsterdam* (1648)

❖ ❖ ❖

They all drink here, from the moment they are able to lick a spoon. The women of the neighborhood entertain each other with a pipe and brazier; young and old, they all smoke.

—*Nicasius de Sille, from a letter home to the Netherlands* (1653)

❖ ❖ ❖

I may say, & say truly, that if there be any terrestrial happiness to be had by people of all ranks, especially of an inferior rank, it must certainly be here: here any one may furnish himself with land, & live rent-free.

—*Daniel Denton* (1670)

❖ ❖ ❖

In passing through this island we sometimes encountered such a sweet smell in the air that we stood still.

—*A visiting missionary* (1679)

———————————— ❖ ————————————

Sell New York? Don't think of such a thing! Just give it self-government, and there will be no more trouble.

—*William Penn to the Duke of York* (c. 1683)

❖ ❖ ❖

Here is found Dutch neatness, combined with English taste and architecture; the houses are finished, planned, and painted with the greatest care. . . . Stone being very scarce, nearly the whole town is built of brick.

—*Jean de Crevecoeur* (c. 1770s)

❖ ❖ ❖

The principal street is a noble broad street 100 feet wide called Broadway. It commences at the north gate of the fort by a kind of square or place formerly a parade, now a bowling green railed in, and runs directly in a straight line northeast better than half a mile, where it terminates by another intended square.

—*Thomas Pownall* (mid-1770s)

The town had formerly been built without any regular plan, whence everywhere almost, except what has been rebuilt in consequence of the fire, the streets are small and crooked; the foot-paths, where there are any, narrow, and interrupted by the stairs from the houses, which makes the walking on them extremely inconvenient.

—*The Duke of La Rochefoucauld-Liancourt,*
French refugee (mid-1790s)

❖ ❖ ❖

The beautiful metropolis of America is by no means so clean a city as Boston, but many of its streets have the same characteristics; except that the houses are not quite so fresh-coloured, the sign-boards are not quite so gaudy, the gilded letters not quite so golden, the bricks not quite so red, the stone not quite so white.

—*Charles Dickens* (1842)

❖

The college, tho' only one third of the plan is complete, makes a fine appearance, on one of the finest situations perhaps of any college in the world. Here are taught divinity, mathematics, the practice and theory of medicine, chemistry, surgery, and materia medica. One circumstance I think is a little unlucky, the entrance to this college is thro' one of the streets where the most noted prostitutes live. This is certainly a temptation to the youth that have occasion to pass so often this way.

—*Patrick M'Robert, describing King's College, the future Columbia University* (1774)

❖ ❖ ❖

There is not in any city in the world a finer street than Broadway; it is near a mile in length, and is meant to be still farther extended: it is more than a hundred feet wide from one end to the other. Most parts of the houses are of brick, and a number of them extremely handsome.

—*Duke of La Rochefoucauld-Liancourt* (1799)

❖

The sun will rise this morning upon the greatest experiment in municipal government that the world has ever known—the enlarged city.

—New York Tribune, *on the unification of Manhattan, the Bronx, Queens, Staten Island, and Brooklyn as New York City* (January 1, 1898)

❖ ❖ ❖

By the time the railway is completed, areas that are now given over to rocks and goats will be covered with houses. Plans have already been drawn up by every property owner for the undeveloped real estate at the northern confines of the city which the rapid transit railway is projected to reach.

—*William Barclay Parson, the subway's chief construction engineer* (1900)

❖ ❖ ❖

The great days in New York were just before you got there.

—*Lewis Gannett*

❖

Subways are to New York what water is to the West. Around 1800, nearly all of the city's population was locked into a tiny fraction of its land, clustered at the southern foot of Manhattan island.

—*Jim Dwyer* (1991)

❖ ❖ ❖

While other places tend to get stuck, New York continues to evolve.

—*Karl Lagerfeld*)

❖ ❖ ❖

New York is a present-tense city. It lives in the moment, perhaps because the city's full-blast immediacy engages all the senses simultaneously, squeezing the faculties that allow for reflection on the past and speculation about the future. Like riders on a roller coaster, New Yorkers simply hold on tight.

—*William Grimes* (2009)

Unfortunately there are still people in other areas who regard New York City not as a part of the United States, but as a sort of excrescence fastened to our Eastern shore and peopled by the less venturesome waves of foreigners who failed to go West to the genuine American frontier.

—*Robert Moses* (1956)

5

LADY LIBERTY AND HER "HUDDLED MASSES"

❖

About the only Queen this city has really ever had is the Statue of Liberty.

—*Liz Smith*

❖ ❖ ❖

The details of the lines ought not to arrest the eye . . . the surfaces should be broad and simple, defined by a bold and clear design, accentuated in the important places . . . it should have a summarized character, such as one would give to a rapid sketch.

—*Frederic Auguste Bartholdi, imagining the Statue of Liberty he was designing* (c. 1871)

❖ ❖ ❖

Whoever visits the Statue of Liberty feels that he has come home.

—*An attendant at the Statue of Liberty*

Give me your tired, your poor,
Your huddled masses yearning to be free,
The wretched refuse of your teeming shore,
Send these, the homeless, tempest tossed to me,
I lift my lamp beside the golden door.
　　　　　　—Emma Lazarus ("The Statue of Liberty," 1883)

❖ ❖ ❖

There could hardly be a finer site for the Statue of Liberty, and it is not easy in New York to escape her matronly benediction. Like the headmaster's wife at the beginning of the term, she greets you inexorably as you sail in through the harbor, and keeps her eye on you throughout.
　　　　　　　　　　　　　　　—Jan Morris (1969)

❖ ❖ ❖

For the Fujianese, there are only two places in America. There is New York City; then there is everywhere else.
　　　　　　　　　　　　　　　　—Jennifer 8. Lee

With the very symbol of liberty, that stupid giant female, with her illuminating torch, becomes a monster of hated men, her torch a club that ominously threatens us: Get to work! Get to work!

—*James Huneker* (1915)

❖ ❖ ❖

The ghost of the Mayflower pilots every immigrant ship, and Ellis Island is another name for Plymouth Rock.

—*Mary Antin* (1914)

❖ ❖ ❖

Though in fact it played its historic role for only half a century, nearly every Italian, Polish, German, or Russian American one meets claims that his grandfather or great-grandfather came through Ellis Island—an earthier, and rather more convincing, parallel to the claim that one's forebears came over, or were even born, upon the *Mayflower*.

—*Jan Morris* (1969)

They had heard of New York as a place vague and far away, a city that, like Heaven, to them had existed by faith alone. All the days of their lives they had heard of it, and it seemed to them the centre of all the glory, all the wealth, and all the freedom of the world. New York. It had an alluring sound. Who would know them there? Who would look down upon them?

—*Paul Laurence Dunbar* (1901)

❖ ❖ ❖

Years ago it was "the brutal and uncouth Irish"; then it was the "knife-wielding" Italians; later it was the "clannish" Jews with "strange" ways; yesterday it was the Negro; today it is the Puerto Ricans—and the Negroes—who are relegated to the last rung of New York's social ladder.

—*Jesus Colon* (1961)

❖ ❖ ❖

Puerto Ricans . . . they hit New York in the 1940s, the wrong time. But like when is it right, when your face don't help, your accent ain't French, and your clothes don't fit?

—*Edwin Torres*

One may find for the asking an Italian, a German, a French, African, Spanish, Bohemian, Russian, Scandinavian, Jewish, and Chinese colony. The one thing you shall vainly ask for in the chief city of America is a distinctively American community. There is none; certainly not among the tenements.

—*Jacob Riis* (1890)

6
The Melting Pot, Salad Bowl, Stir-Fry

New York, with its novel, varied, and ever-changing features, is calculated to leave a very marked impression on a stranger's mind. In one part, one can suppose it to be a negro town; in another, a German city; while a strange dreamy resemblance to Liverpool pervades the whole.

—*Isabella Bird* (1854)

❖ ❖ ❖

New York will achieve its position—it has achieved the position it has—rather by in- than by exclusiveness, and it is good that there should be a place where all sorts of foreignesses—all sorts—should be united as it were in a common frame.

—*Ford Madox Ford* (1927)

What, indeed, is a New Yorker? Is he Jew or Irish? Is he English or German? Is he Russian or Polish? He may be something of all these, and yet he is wholly none of them. . . . New York, indeed, resembles a magic cauldron.

—*Charles Whibley* (1908)

❖ ❖ ❖

It has been said that New York is not part of America. That may be true. . . . But it is the fire under the boiling pot, and, as Jimmy Durante might paraphrase, I doubt if America could get along without New York.

—*Carlos Romulo* (1943)

❖ ❖ ❖

New York is a cosmopolitan city; but it is not a city of cosmopolitans. Most of the masses in New York have a nation, whether or not it be the nation to which New York belongs. Those who are Americanised are American, and very patriotically American.

—*G. K. Chesterton* (1921)

Many Italians hardly know they are outside their native land, because here they have everything Italian: friends, churches, schools, theater, banks, businesses, daily papers, societies, meeting places. And they can travel for many kilometers without hearing spoken any language except the Italian, or Italian dialect.

—*Arnaldo Fraccaroli* (1931))

❖ ❖ ❖

Djellabas flapping in the wind, two men leave a Yemeni café, holding the tiny cups of tea like bowsprits before them. They cross Atlantic Avenue, which is a hill where it intersects with Court Avenue, looking west toward New York harbor, New Jersey, and the rest of America.

—*Robert Sullivan* (2008)

The men on that corner in Kensington, just like the people I had known throughout my life, were immigrants in the most complete sense of the word—their loyalties still firmly attached to the countries they had left one, five, or twenty years earlier. If there was one thing I admired most about them, it was that they had succeeded, at least partly, in re-creating in Brooklyn some of what they had lost when they left their countries of origin.

—*Dinaw Mengestu* (2008)

❖ ❖ ❖

No easy generalization about the Germans or the Italians or about any other division of New York's foreign stock can be true. A man renounces his country and swears allegiance to another, but nobody can say how deep the old patriotism went, how long it will persist, how it will affect his life, and the life of his children.

—*Robert Waithman* (1940)

If you live in New York, even if you're Catholic, you're Jewish.

—Lenny Bruce

❖ ❖ ❖

Their uneasiness and fear were even reflected in their attitude toward the children they had given birth to in this country. They referred to those like myself, the little Brooklyn-born Bajans (Barbadians), as "these New York children," and complained that they couldn't discipline us properly because of the laws here.

—*Paule Marshall* (1994)

❖ ❖ ❖

As we cross the crowded, filthy, immigrant street, now black and Puerto Rican instead of Jewish and Italian, she marvels at how changed it all is. I tell her nothing has changed, only the color of the people and the language spoken. The hungry, angling busy-ness of Delancey Street . . . is all still in place.

—*Vivian Gornick* (1987)

New York confronts the incoming tides of art with a broad gesture of acceptance. Symbolists from Prague, Ukrainian wood-sculptors, performers on unheard-of instruments from recently discovered countries, practitioners of every known and unknown variety of art, even historians from England—each and all are assured of welcome.

—*Philip Guedalla* (1927)

❖ ❖ ❖

In kindergarten, when we learned about Ellis Island we were taught that America was a melting pot—everything blended together into one massive swirling pool. . . . By the time I got to middle school, that analogy had fallen out of favor. . . . America had become a tossed salad.

—*Jennifer 8. Lee* (2008)

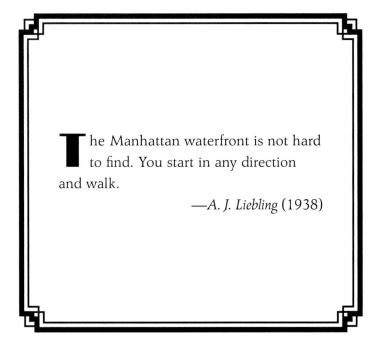

The Manhattan waterfront is not hard to find. You start in any direction and walk.

—*A. J. Liebling* (1938)

7
THE SHAPE OF THINGS

Situated on an island which I think it will one day cover, it rises like Venice from the sea, and like that fairest of cities in the days of her glory, receives into its lap tribute of all the riches of the earth.

—*Frances Trollope* (1827)

❖ ❖ ❖

Divided into Lower Bay and Upper Bay, the Harbor is like a giant hourglass. Through its neck, the Narrows, the sand- and refuse-laden tides ebb and flow.

—*New York Panorama* (1938)

❖ ❖ ❖

The borders—the East River and the Hudson are inaccessible! . . . Well, the sea and the vast rivers are invisible and no one gets the benefit of their beauty, their spaciousness, their movement, the splendid play of light on the water! New York, an immense seaport, is as landlocked for its inhabitants as Moscow!

—*Le Corbusier* (1936)

Do you realize that one can't look in any direction in Manhattan without seeing water at the end of the street: the Harbor, the Hudson and East Rivers, the Narrows, and even the Atlantic. Here we are entering the age of Aquarius, the age of water, with New York the wateriest city in the entire world. Yet we, who could be beachcombers on a dozen exciting waterfronts, live here as if we were in the middle of the Sahara!

—*Helen Hayes* (1972)

❖ ❖ ❖

Unlike most cities on navigable water, New York faces inward toward Central Park and the mainland as much as it faces outward to the harbor and the rest of the world. This simultaneous facing inward and outward is true of its citizens as well.

—*Kenneth T. Jackson and David S. Dunbar* (2002)

The shape of Manhattan island was like that of a sole, with its head being in Harlem, and its tail at the Castle garden: the backbone being represented by Broadway, and the continuous line of ships fringing the wharves along the East River and the Hudson River respectively, figuring the lateral small bones of the fish.

—*G. A. Sala* (1882)

❖ ❖ ❖

A little strip of an island with a row of well-fed folks up and down the middle, and a lot of hungry folks on each side.

—*Harry L. Wilson* (1902)

❖ ❖ ❖

The George Washington Bridge over the Hudson is the most beautiful bridge in the world. Made of cables and steel beams, it gleams in the sky like a reversed arch. It is blessed. It is the only seat of grace in the disordered city. It is painted an aluminum color and, between water and sky, you see nothing but the bent cord supported by two steel towers.

—*Le Corbusier* (1936)

New York City is made up of five boroughs, four of which—Brooklyn, Queens, Richmond, the Bronx—compose like crinkled lily pads about the basking trout of Manhattan.

—*New York Panorama* (1938)

❖ ❖ ❖

To the traveler by air, especially from the north or east, the city appears with the instancy of revelation: the slowly crinkling samite of its rivers and New York Harbor vaporous beyond, the Bronx splayed out and interwoven with the tight dark Hudson Valley foliage, Brooklyn and Queens and Staten Island dispersed in their enormous encampments about the narrow seaward-thrusting rock of Manhattan.

—*Vincent McHugh* (1938)

On the map, the central borough of Manhattan, about twelve and a half miles long and two and a half miles at its extreme width, looks like a small stone cleaver about to hack at the huge loaf of Long Island.

—*New York Panorama* (1938)

❖ ❖ ❖

As much as its skyline has been photographed, New York is a city fetishistically shown from above, by both the media and artists. . . . We need to get on top to get perspective, to lose perspective, to feel in control, to feel awed, to feel free as the camera flies over the tip of the Chrysler Building.

—*Stacia J. N. Decker* (2009)

❖ ❖ ❖

A hundred times I have thought: New York is a catastrophe, and fifty times: it is a beautiful catastrophe.

—*Le Corbusier* (1936)

Let us divide the land of the peninsula of Manhattan in equal rectangular lots, where the streets will reach from the Hudson to the East River; perpendicularly, throughout the entire length of the city, may be traced avenues. Let us make away with the use of sonorous names; let us number them from south to north; let the avenues be counted from one to ten, the fifth serving to divide the east and the west of the city. In this manner all will become clear and arithmetical.

—*Jean Schopfer* (1902)

❖ ❖ ❖

I wondered how this town ever got put together. Some guy was dreaming big all right. Starting down in Wall Street and nosing ever upward into the ruins of the old West Side, Broadway snakes through the island, the only curve in this world of grids. . . . Broadway is the moulting python of strict New York.

—*Martin Amis* (1985)

As a later *Batman* editor perspicaciously noted, Gotham is New York's noirish side—"Manhattan below Fourteenth Street at 3 a.m., November 28 in a cold year"—whereas Superman's Metropolis presents New York's cheerier face, "Manhattan between Fourteenth and One Hundred and Tenth Streets on the brightest, sunniest July day of the year."
—*Edwin G. Burrows and Mike Wallace*

❖ ❖ ❖

Over a period of two centuries and more, Manhattan's face has been lifted and relifted unceasingly. Abrupt ledges of rock have been levelled, deep narrow valleys filled, forests cleared. . . . As the city expanded, miles of similar swampland in Brooklyn, Queens and Harlem have been reclaimed to provide space for buildings and homes.
—*New York Panorama* (1938)

This great, plunging, dramatic, ferocious, swift, and terrible big city is the most folksy and provincial place I have lived in. New York is the biggest collection of villages in the world.

—Alistair Cooke (1952)

❖ ❖ ❖

So complete is each neighborhood, and so strong the sense of neighborhood, that many a New Yorker spends a lifetime within the confines of an area smaller than a country village. Let him walk two blocks from his corner, and he is in a strange land and will feel uneasy till he gets back.

—E. B. White (1949)

❖ ❖ ❖

Some New York streets have Mayors, but they are not elected. A man lives on a street until the mayoralty grows over him, like a patina.

—A. J. Liebling (1938)

I had the typical cliché attitude toward New York City: that it's tough, and I was gonna have to tough out three weeks down here. It turns out that it's a nicer Village than the one I live in in Vermont.

—*Billy Romp, Christmas-tree vendor, quoted by Mitchell Duneier* (1995)

❖ ❖ ❖

New York is like a country, the neighborhood is your town, you spot someone from the block or the building in another neighborhood and the first impulse to the brain is, What are *you* doing here?

—*Vivian Gornick* (1996)

❖ ❖ ❖

There are certainly numberless women of fashion who consider it perfectly natural to go miles down Fifth Avenue, or Madison Avenue, yet for whom a voyage of a half a dozen blocks east or west would be an adventure, almost a dangerous impairment of good breeding.

—*Jules Romains* (1941)

[In New York] most men's ambition is to live in a house with a "brown stone *front*." It is called brown stone, but is of a reddish chocolate color, and is one of the handsomest stones I know. No matter what the rest of the house is built of—wood, brick, or plaster and daub—it must have a stone front, and *look* like a stone building.

—*Therese Yelverton* (1875)

❖ ❖ ❖

The Lower East Side's current inhabitants, despite their fascination with the louche, are educated and middle-class, with mothers back on Long Island wishing their guitar-playing daughters had gone to medical school.

—*Cynthia Ozick* (2000)

❖ ❖ ❖

Take in imagination such a bird's-eye view of the city of New York as might be had from a balloon. The houses are climbing heavenward—then, twelve, even fifteen stories, tier on tier of people living one family above another.

—*Henry George* (c. 1883)

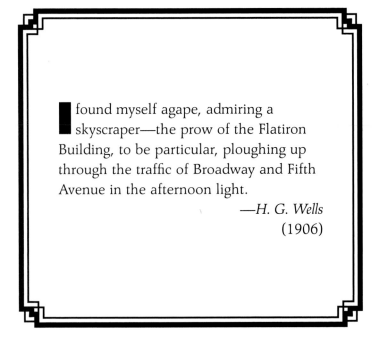

I found myself agape, admiring a skyscraper—the prow of the Flatiron Building, to be particular, ploughing up through the traffic of Broadway and Fifth Avenue in the afternoon light.

—*H. G. Wells*
(1906)

8
Skyscraping New York

❖

This is the first sensation of life in New York—you feel that the Americans have practically added a new dimension to space. They move almost as much on the perpendicular as on the horizontal plane. When they find themselves a little crowded, they simply tip a street on end and call it a skyscraper.

—William Archer (1899)

❖ ❖ ❖

One could believe that giants had built this city for giants, and if you walk in lower Broadway among these monsters, you get the illusion of being in a deep mountain canyon.

—*Ludwig Fulda* (1913)

❖ ❖ ❖

It is only little by little, as you grow used to this enormity, that you reach comfort in New York, that you look casually at the Equitable Building, and contemptuously at the little apartments houses of eight floors.

—*Philip Gibbs* (1919)

Skyscrapers are the first thing which a foreigner sees when he comes to America. The dizzy loftiness of the Manhattan skyline looms like a citadel raised on high by the Cyclops.

—*Arthur Feiler* (1928)

❖ ❖ ❖

The skyscrapers looked like tall gravestones. I wondered why, if the United States was so rich, as surely it is, did its biggest city look so grotesque?

—*Bernardo Vega*

❖ ❖ ❖

These skyscrapers, who belong to a brotherhood of giants, help each other to rise, to prop each other up, to soar until all sense of perspective disappears. You try to count the stories one by one, then your weary gaze starts to climb in tens.

—*Paul Morand* (New York, 1929)

❖

If 1,668,172 people . . . are to be set down in one narrow strip of land between two quiet rivers, you can hardly improve on this solid mass of buildings and the teeming organism of human life that streams through them.

—*Brooks Atkinson* (1964)

❖ ❖ ❖

The Empire State Building is the lighthouse of Manhattan.

—*Robert A. M. Stern*

❖ ❖ ❖

Manhattan has been compelled to expand skyward because of the absence of any other direction in which to grow.

—*E. B. White* (1949)

❖ ❖ ❖

The skyscraper is not a plume rising from the face of the city. It has been made that, and wrongly. The plume was a poison to the city. The skyscraper is an instrument. A magnificent instrument for the concentration of population, for getting rid of land congestion, for classification, for internal efficiency.

—*Le Corbusier* (1936)

The staired and serried skyscrapers of Manhattan, rising from the bay to rival the Cathedrals and Great White Thrones of the National Parks in beauty and grandeur, are made possible by a tough bed of rock, Manhattan schist: a thick, unyielding, coarsely crystalline rock glinting with mica.

—*New York Panorama* (1938)

❖ ❖ ❖

Look at the Manhattan skyline and you will see a smoothly blended city. The beauty of its individual architecture is not surpassed anywhere in the world. Remember that New York is a constantly growing city, and that it has an architectural theme all its own. . . . I would call it a patchwork of beauty.

—*Fiorello La Guardia*
("Ten Misconceptions of New York," 1939)

The skyscrapers, these great presses of humanity, disgorge their exhausted contents. . . . At the foot of the buildings the revolving doors are whirling like crazy wheels, each fan blowing out human beings on to the sidewalk.

—*Paul Morand* (New York, 1929)

❖ ❖ ❖

Skyscraper national park.

—*Kurt Vonnegut* (1976)

❖ ❖ ❖

New York is a stone garden. Stone plants send up stems of varying height . . . a jungle where cathedrals and Greek temples balance on stilts.

—*Jean Cocteau*

❖ ❖ ❖

A city like this makes one dream tall and feel in on things.

—*Toni Morrison* (1992)

At night the white glow that fizzes upward from the city—an inverted electric Niagara—obscures the stars, and except for the Planetarium's windowless mimicry, New York is oblivious of the cosmos.

—*Cynthia Ozick* (2000)

❖ ❖ ❖

I never found them offensive or overbearing, neither did I love them; they didn't invite dislike, they were too polite, eight-hundred-pound gorillas in tuxes, having no need to beat their chests. . . . They were at once the most dominant and least assuming facet of the New York skyline: Don't mind me, they said.

—*Philip Lopate* (2002)

The most permanent feature of New York is undoubtedly its air of self-importance, the locally prized conviction that, when you're here, you're in the place to be.

—*Guy Trebay* (1994)

9
Customs, Manners, and Mannerisms

❖

The tension between public and private may well be the
most confrontational of all tensions in the coming century.
New York City has much to teach America about how to live
with these tensions in a productive and realistic manner.
            —*Kenneth T. Jackson and David S. Dunbar* (2002)

❖ ❖ ❖

With all the opulence and splendor of this city, there
is very little good breeding to be found. We have been
treated with an assiduous respect; but I have not seen one
real gentleman, one well-bred man, since I came to town.
            —*John Adams* (1774)

❖ ❖ ❖

[Though] the majority are descended from runaway
vagabonds expelled from other places, yet they are so
stuck up and make such display, especially in New York,
as perhaps nowhere else on earth.
            —*A Hessian British soldier's letter to his brother, during the*
            Revolutionary War (June 24, 1777)

❖

New York and Philadelphia dislike one another with an indescribable hatred. If Philadelphia should become extinct, everybody in New York would rejoice, and vice versa. New York is the vilest of cities, write the Philadelphia journalists. In New York, they speak no better of Philadelphia.

—*Dietrich von Bulow, German visitor* (1790s)

❖ ❖ ❖

Upon the whole, a walk through New York will disappoint an Englishman: there is, on the surface of society, a carelessness, a laziness, an unsocial indifference, which freezes the blood and disgusts the judgment.

—*Henry B. Fearon* (1819)

❖ ❖ ❖

You Gothamites strain hard to attain a metropolitan character, but I think if you *felt* very metropolitan you would not be showing it on all occasions.

—*James Russell Lowell* (1844)

An American store is generally a very extensive apartment, handsomely decorated, the roof frequently supported on marble pillars. The owner or clerk is seen seated by his goods, absorbed in the morning paper . . . He deigns to answer your inquiries, but, in place of the pertinacious perseverance with which an English shopman displays his wares, it seems a matter of perfect indifference to the American whether you purchase or not.

—*Isabella Bird* (1854)

❖ ❖ ❖

This is New York and there's no law against being annoying.

—*William Kuntsler*

❖ ❖ ❖

In the summer evenings the whole indoor population of New York seems to overflow on to the "stoops" of their house.

—*Mary Duffus Hardy* (1881)

On Fourth Street you could tell when a window was open because someone was almost always framed in it, leaning on a small pillow and usually yelling into the street or to a neighbor a floor or two above or below.

—*Jerome Weidman* (1939)

❖ ❖ ❖

The railway guard, the waiter, the cabdriver—these are the men upon whose care the comfort of the stranger depends in every land. . . . In New York, then, you are met everywhere by a sort of urbane familiarity. The man who does you a service, for which you pay him, is neither civil nor uncivil. He contrives, in a way which is by no means unpleasant, to put himself on an equality with you.

—*Charles Whibley* (1908)

Every man Jack when he first sets foot on the stones of Manhattan has got to fight. He has got to fight at once until either he or his adversary wins. There is no resting between rounds, for there are no rounds. It is slugging from the first. It is a fight to the finish.

—*O. Henry* (1910)

❖ ❖ ❖

Its magazines go everywhere, standardizing ideas; its slang invades the remotest receses, standardizing speech; its melodies are in every home, standardizing entertainment; the very thought of Broadway, the Main Street of all America, thrills millions who are scattered far and wide.

—*J. A. Spender* (Through British Eyes, 1928)

❖ ❖ ❖

New York is not America, but it is plain to all beholders that all America would like to be New York.

—*Yvon Lapaquellerie* (1929)

❖

New York City has been to the United States what America has been to the rest of the world, the great experiment in multicultural re-creation.

—*Kenneth T. Jackson and David S. Dunbar* (2002)

❖ ❖ ❖

I fled New England and came to Manhattan, that island off the coast of America, where human nature was king and everyone exuded character and had a big attitude.

—*Spaulding Gray*

❖ ❖ ❖

There is nothing distinctive about living in New York; over eight million other people are doing it.

—*Don Herold* (1988)

❖ ❖ ❖

As soon as you feel you understand New York, an unpalatable fact becomes apparent: your understanding is obsolete.

—*John Gattuso*

New Yorkers are modest. It is a distinction for a child in New York to be the brightest on one block; he acquires no exaggerated idea of his own relative intelligence. Prairie geniuses are raced in cheap company when young. They are intoxicated by the feeling of being boy wonders in Amarillo, and when they bounce off New York's skin as adults they resent it.

—*A. J. Liebling*

❖ ❖ ❖

Being a New Yorker is never having to say you're sorry.
—*Lily Tomlin* (1992)

❖ ❖ ❖

It is a city filled with preening show-offs, anxious that someone is looking at them and equally anxious that no one is looking at them.

—*Thomas Beller* (2009)

Unlike Bartleby, downtown's most distinctive imaginary inhabitant, New York never prefers not to. New York prefers and prefers and prefers—it prefers power and scope to tranquility and intimacy, it prefers struggle and steel to acquiescence and cushions.

—*Cynthia Ozick* (2000)

❖ ❖ ❖

Someone wants your attention. He is a New York character, and the encounter is one most New Yorkers have had at one time or another. A stranger approaches you on the street and starts talking. It's not entirely clear what he wants, but his speech is rapid and urgent. He tells you his name, though it occurs to you that it may not be his real name. You nod, you look at your watch, you keep walking, quickening your pace, instinctively checking the placement of your wallet or purse. Is he panhandling? Threatening? Is he lost? Crazy?

—*A. O. Scott*

Rudeness is the privacy of New Yorkers.

—*Thomas Griffith* (1956)

❖ ❖ ❖

The citizens of New York are tolerant not only from disposition but from necessity. The city has to be tolerant, otherwise it would explode in a radioactive cloud of hate and rancor and bigotry.

—*E. B. White* (1949)

❖ ❖ ❖

Now there may be people who move easily into New York without travail, but most I have talked to about it have had some kind of trial by torture before acceptance. And the acceptance is a double thing. It seems to me that the city finally accepts you just as you finally accept the city.

—*John Steinbeck*

The Yankees perfectly represented what might be called the New York Idea, which held that New York had and was the best of everything. No matter what line of work a man was in—finance, industry, communications, the arts, sports, or fashion—he was not really *in* unless he was in New York.

—*Bruce Catton*

❖ ❖ ❖

At this time [c. 1966] in the Bronx we walked in a distinctive way that we called bopping. A young man who "bopped" told the world that he was street tough, prepared to fight if challenged. The "bop" consisted of a slight dip on one leg as you walked, arms swinging, fingers held stiff and pointing slightly to the rear, head held slightly to one side.

—*Geoffrey Canada*

When it's hot, New Yorkers get hot under the collar. What pisses us off the most is being robbed of our urban cool. Step out of doors on any Manhattan dog day and no matter who or what you are, everything crisp and businesslike about you soon becomes damp, limp, and clingy.

—*Lee Stringer* (1985)

❖ ❖ ❖

The term New Yorker is as much a verb as a noun. Unlike most places that demand a certain elapsed time period before one is considered a native, New York is democratic. If you can talk the talk and walk the walk, you are a New Yorker.

—*Kenneth T. Jackson and David S. Dunbar* (2002)

❖ ❖ ❖

I myself have the right to become a *New Yorker*, if I am strong enough to cut a furrow in New York. I should not thereby become an American.

—*Le Corbusier* (1936)

--- ❖ ---

New York kids, from penthouse to welfare hotel, from shtetl to ghetto, are little shock troops of contemporary urban life, taking for granted the extremes of the city into which they are born and dramatizing those extremes with their unquestioning adaptation.

—*Michele Landsberg* (1989)

❖ ❖ ❖

Where we live, in New York City, just having a wife and children is considered a bit quaint. I sometimes think that someday we might be put on the Grayline Tour of Greenwich Village as a nuclear family.

—*Calvin Trillin*

❖ ❖ ❖

New York is simply a distillation of the entire United States, the most of everything, the conclusive proof that there is an American civilization. New York is casual, intellectual, subtle, effective, and devastatingly witty.

—*Raymond Loewy*

Educationally, New York is to the United States what Paris is to France. . . . Whoever seeks intellectual stimulation will find it in America's first city.

—*Sidney Hook*

❖ ❖ ❖

Like millions of iron filings, people stream to magnetic New York, and their mere presence in one place is a million-fold mutual confirmation: to be there is to have arrived somewhere central and magnificent. So much haste, ambition, and urgency pour through the streets that you can't but feel a vicarious intensity.

—*Michele Landsberg* (1989)

❖ ❖ ❖

The true New Yorker does not really seek information about the outside world. He feels that if anything is not in New York it is not likely to be interesting.

—*Aubrey Menen*

❖

It is a city of love and compassion and hundreds of thousands of unsung and uncelebrated acts of charity and kindness and heroism every minute of every hour and every hour of every day.

—*Mayor Robert F. Wagner, Jr.*

❖ ❖ ❖

If we are to look to a city that most realistically maintains and yet questions fundamental American traits and provides an arena where those can be honestly confronted and questioned, it is New York.

—*Kenneth T. Jackson and David S. Dunbar* (2002)

Wall Street, the New World's "hell," where more fortunes have been made and lost in one year of the last four than in the centuries of the lives of other countries.

—*George T. Borrett* (1864)

10

MONEY TALKS

I cannot sufficiently wonder at the lazy unconcern of many persons, both farmers and others, who are willing enough to draw their rations and pay in return for doing almost nothing.

—*Isaack de Rasieres, letter home to Holland from New Amsterdam* (c. 1626)

❖ ❖ ❖

Formerly New Netherland was never spoken of, and now heaven and earth seem to be stirred up by it and every one tries to be the first in selecting the best pieces [of land] there.

—*Letter from the directors of the West India Company to Peter Stuyvesant* (c. 1649)

❖ ❖ ❖

The town is seated . . . commodiously for trades, and that is their chief employment, for they plant and sow little.

—*Anonymous English visitor* (1661)

❖

No gold or silver circulates here, but beads, which
the Indians make and call seawant. . . . We can buy
everything with it and gladly take it in payment.

—Nicasius de Sille, from a letter home
to the Netherlands (1654)

❖ ❖ ❖

The price of provisions fluctuates here exceedingly . . .
and persons who know how to take opportunities may
furnish themselves very cheap; after refusing to buy at
their price, I was soon after asked by the same persons,
what would I give?

—Henry Wansey (1794)

❖ ❖ ❖

Every thought, word, look, and action of the multitude
seemed to be absorbed by commerce.

—John Lambert (1807)

In spite of the declaration of the venerable Franklin [that] "three removes are as bad as a fire," the inhabitants of New York are the most locomotive people on the face of the earth. This movable propensity appears to be partly caused by a progressive state of prosperity; for, as the value of property in this city has always been steadily increasing, the owners are unwilling to grant leases, hoping each successive year to add materially to their rent rolls.

—*James Boardman* (1830)

❖ ❖ ❖

In fifty years the population of New York has increased tenfold, its wealth probably a hundredfold. . . . [The] merit belongs chiefly to the industry, the capital, the intelligence, and the enterprise of that, numerically speaking, insignificant minority of Wall Street and Pearl Street.

—*Michel Chevalier*

Could I begin again, knowing what I know now, I would buy every foot of land on the island of Manhattan.

—*John Jacob Astor* (c. 1840)

❖ ❖ ❖

Our good city of New York has already arrived at the state of society to be found in the large cities of Europe; overburdened with population, and where the two extremes of costly luxury in living, expensive establishments, and improvident waste are presented in daily and hourly contrast with squalid misery and hopeless destitution.

—*Philip Hone* (1847)

❖ ❖ ❖

The American seems always in a hurry and excited; at his meals, in his study, and at his counter. For example, in the morning hours, when the New York business population, old and young—and all is business in New York—pours out into the main artery, in Broadway, and descends hurriedly "down town," nothing in the world could stop or divert the torrent.

—*Adam de Gurowski, Polish revolutionary* (1849)

New Yorkers seem to live to make money and spend it.
Fortunes are not the rule, for money is seldom hoarded,
but spent in the same reckless way in which it is made.
There is little inducement to a man to put by money.
To be much thought of, a New Yorker must be in trade.
Merchants are thought more of than lawyers and medical
men, while those who do nothing, be they rich as
Croesus, are thought little of at all.

—*Anonymous English traveler* (c. 1860)

❖ ❖ ❖

I have never walked down Fifth Avenue without thinking
of money. I have never walked there with a companion
without talking of it. I fancy that every man there, in
order to maintain the spirit of the place, should bear
on his forehead a label stating how many dollars he is
worth, and that every label should be expected to assert a
falsehood.

—*Anthony Trollope* (1862)

What can New York—noisy, roaring, rumbling, tumbling, bustling, stormy, turbulent New York—have to do with silence? Amid the universal clatter, the incessant din of business, the all-swallowing vortex of the great money whirlpool . . . who has any . . . idea . . . of silence?

—*Walt Whitman*

❖ ❖ ❖

Nothing is given to beauty; everything centers in hard utility. It is the outward expression of the freest, fiercest individualism. The very houses are alive with the instinct of competition, and strain each one to overtop its neighbors.

—*George W. Steevens* (1896)

❖ ❖ ❖

A strange craziness is abroad in the land. Some mysterious spirit of evil has led our people into the blindest, wildest infatuation . . . At least half the people are living beyond their means.

—New York weekly *Round Table* (1866)

❖

[The] very first of the Ten Commandments of New York: "Thou Shalt Not Be Poor!"

—*Joaquin Miller* (1886)

❖ ❖ ❖

Uncharitableness and lack of generosity have never been New York failings; the citizens are keenly sensible to any real, tangible distress or need. A blizzard in Dakota, an earthquake in South Carolina, a flood in Pennsylvania—after any such catastrophe hundreds of thousands of dollars are raised in New York at a day's notice.

—*Theodore Roosevelt* (1891)

❖ ❖ ❖

Mammon, n. The god of the world's leading religion. His chief temple is in the holy city of New York.

—*Ambrose Bierce* (1906)

New York City is the most fatally fascinating thing in America. She sits like a great witch at the gate of the country, showing her alluring white face and hiding her crooked hands and feet under the folds of her wide garments—constantly enticing thousands from far within, and tempting those who come from across the seas to go no farther. And all these become the victims of her caprice.

—*James Weldon Johnson* (1912)

❖ ❖ ❖

When I had looked at the lights of Broadway by night, I made to my American friends an innocent remark that seemed for some reason to amuse them. I had looked, not without joy, at that long kaleidoscope of coloured lights arranged in large letters and sprawling trade-marks, advertising everything from pork to pianos. . . . I said to them, in my simplicity, "What a glorious garden of wonders this would be, to any one who was lucky enough to be unable to read."

—*G. K. Chesterton* (1921)

Out of the tenements Cold as stone,
Dark figures start for work,
I watch them sadly shuffle on,
'Tis dawn, dawn in New York.

—*Claude McKay*
("When Dawn Comes to the City," 1922)

❖ ❖ ❖

"Don't get much time to sleep," said a Broadway soda clerk. "I have to sleep so fast I'm all tired out when I get up in the morning."

—*Vincent McHugh* (1938)

❖ ❖ ❖

That sinister Stonehenge of economic man, Rockefeller Center.

—*Cyril Connolly*

The chief industry in my part of the country is getting by. You can get by in several million ways. I know a professional faster and a professional eater, and both were getting by all right when I last saw them.

—*A. J. Liebling* (1938)

❖ ❖ ❖

The trouble with New York is it's so convenient to everything I can't afford.

—*Jack Barry* (1952)

❖ ❖ ❖

[New Yorkers] make more, sell more, buy more, eat more and enjoy more than the citizens of any other city in the world.

—*Mayor Robert F. Wagner, Jr.*

Anyone who has ever struggled with poverty knows how extremely expensive it is to be poor; and if one is a member of a captive population, economically speaking, one's feet have simply been placed on the treadmill forever. One is victimized, economically, in a thousand ways—rent, for example, or car insurance. Go shopping one day in Harlem—for anything—and compare Harlem prices and quality with those downtown.

—*James Baldwin* (1960)

❖ ❖ ❖

The only people who can afford to live in New York are the rich and the poor.

—*David McGlynn*

❖ ❖ ❖

It is often said that New York is a city for only the rich and the very poor. It is less often said that New York is also, at least for those of us who came there from somewhere else, a city for only the very young.

—*Joan Didion* (1968)

Neighborhoods accumulate personalities. Park Avenue still means rich, West End Avenue still means bourgeois. When I think of uptown I think of class.

—*Vivian Gornick* (1996)

❖ ❖ ❖

There's a right and a wrong side of the tracks in every city; but in New York what floor you live on, which direction your apartment faces, says a tremendous amount about who you are.

—Steven Gaines

❖ ❖ ❖

To us, the Yankees were a Manhattan team, not a Bronx team. I know they were called the Bronx Bombers, but I looked upon them as being elitists from Manhattan. We were the workers, and they were the elites, the aristocracy.

—*Brooklyn Borough President Marty Markowitz* (2008)

What New York had more of than anywhere was economic diversity. If it took big amounts of steel or coal, New York couldn't produce it. But the first stage of practically any product could be created here, and New York led America in patents, in innovation, in product design and creativity.

—*Robert Fitch* (1993)

❖ ❖ ❖

Among New Yorkers, it is practically an article of faith that anyone who runs what seems to be a small seasonal business—the ice-cream man in the park, for instance—can be found on any cold day in February casually blowing hundreds of dollars at some Florida dog track.

—*Calvin Trillin* (1994)

The unit of exchange on Canal Street is the dallah. Dallahs are dollars crossbred with dinars, pesos, yen, dirhams, zlotys, rubles, piastres. Salesmen in storefronts and sidewalk venders who know almost no other English yell "Fifty dallah!" and "T'ree dallah!" and "Ten dallah!" up and down the streets. Dollars often exist only on paper on video display terminals; dallahs are always real.

—*Ian Frazier* (1990)

❖ ❖ ❖

There's a store, it seems, to serve every quirk of the immense population. Near our apartment, a boutique specializes in matching jewelry for dog owners and their pets; another, Tender Buttons (name stolen from Gertrude Stein), sells nothing but exotic and antique buttons.

—*Michele Landsberg* (1989)

Whoever is Mayor of New York is the biggest man in town, welcome everywhere. He is also the most picked upon—the man who gets the blame when *anything* goes wrong.

—Warren Moscow

11
LEADING MEN

I shall govern you as a father his children, for the advantage of the chartered West India Company, and these burghers, and this land.

—*Peter Stuyvesant, on his inauguration as New Netherland's director general* (1647)

❖ ❖ ❖

These persons had been good and dear friends with [Stuyvesant] always, and he, shortly before, had regarded them as the most honorable, able, intelligent and pious men of the country, yet as soon as they did not follow the General's wishes they were this and that, some of them rascals, liars, rebels, usurers and spendthrifts, in a word, hanging was almost too good for them.

—*Van der Donck, of his former friend Peter Stuyvesant, the director general of New Netherland* (1648)

No Caliph, Khan or Caesar has risen to power or opulence more rapidly than Tweed I. Ten years ago this monarch was pursuing the humble occupation of a chairmaker in an obscure street in this city. He now rules the State as Napoleon ruled France, or as the Medici ruled Florence.

—*Louis J. Jennings* (1870)

❖ ❖ ❖

Let's stop them damned pictures! I don't care much what the papers write about me—my constituents can't read. But—dammit!—they can see pictures!

—*William Marcy "Boss" Tweed, of Tammany Hall,
the Democratic party political power,
regarding Thomas Nast's drawings in* Harper's (1871)

Holding high public office, honored and respected by large classes of the community in which you lived and, I have no doubt, beloved by your associates, you with all these trusts devolved upon you, with all the opportunity you had, by the faithful discharge of your duty, saw fit to pervert the powers with which you were clothed in a manner more infamous, more outrageous, than any instance of like character which the history of the civilized world contains!

—*Judge Noah Davis to William Marcy "Boss" Tweed at Tweed's sentencing, "guilty of 102 offences" (1873)*

❖ ❖ ❖

The fact is that New York politics were always dishonest—long before my time. There never was a time when you couldn't buy the board of aldermen. A politician coming forward takes things as they are. . . . I don't think there is ever a fair or honest election in the city of New York.

—*William Marcy "Boss" Tweed (1878)*

We have a real police commissioner. His teeth are big and white, his eyes are small and piercing, his voice is rasping. He makes our policemen feel as the little froggies did when the stork came to rule them. His heart is full of reform and a policeman in a full uniform, with helmet, revolver and nightclub, is no more to him than a plain, everyday human being.

—*Arthur Brisbane on Theodore Roosevelt* (c.1895)

❖ ❖ ❖

I'd rather be a lamppost in New York than Mayor of Chicago.

—*Mayor James J. Walker*

❖ ❖ ❖

There are three things a man must do alone—be born, die, and testify.

—*Mayor Jimmy Walker, on his way to court for his trial* (May 24, 1932)

❖

Fiorello H. La Guardia was alternately a little boy chasing
fire engines or leading a symphony orchestra, and a devoted
Mayor trying to give the people the most for their money.
His tantrums, often genuine, were the noisiest in town, for
he was determined not to be second best in anything.

—*Warren Moscow* (1967)

❖ ❖ ❖

We aim to rebuild New York, saving what is durable,
what is salvageable, and what is genuinely historical, and
substituting progress for obsolescence.

—*Robert Moses, Parks Commissioner* (c. 1934)

❖ ❖ ❖

[Robert Moses] was both a person and an octopus in
government. . . .He had his finger in the building of
more bridges, tunnels, highways, parkways, parks and
playgrounds, recreation centers, and public as well as
private housing than anyone else in the city's history.

—*Warren Moscow* (1967)

There were times when I was mayor when I wanted to jump. . . . You know, the city's too big. It's too big for one government."

—*Mayor William O'Dwyer,*
quoted by Philip Hamburger (1958)

❖ ❖ ❖

"Mailer, you know you have to be a little insane to run for mayor of this town." Yes you do, I think, and yes, John Lindsay may be a little insane to have tried, but by God I write this to say I hope he wins, John Lindsay, because I think he's okay, in fact, I think he's a great guy, and it would be a miracle if this town had a man for mayor who was okay.

—*Norman Mailer* (1965)

❖ ❖ ❖

The knife of corruption endangered the life of New York City. The scalpel of the law is making us well again.

—*Mayor Ed Koch*
(State of the City address, January 20, 1987)

I have nowhere, at home or abroad, seen so fine a police as the police of New York. . . . On the other hand, the laws for regulation of public vehicles, clearing of streets, and removal of obstructions, are wildly outraged by the people for whose benefit they are intended.

—*Charles Dickens* (1867)

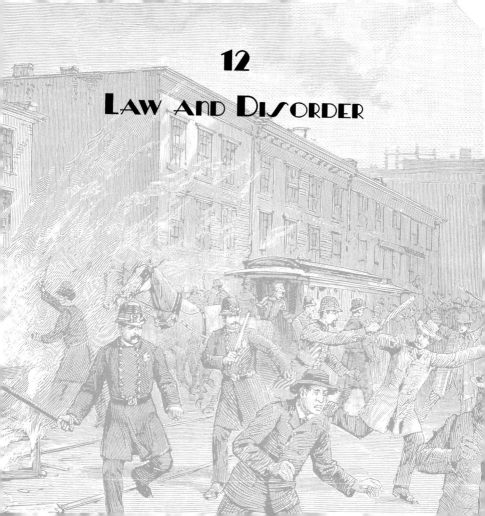

12
LAW AND DISORDER

"Tell me, what is the power base in this town?" "If you mean who runs New York, the answer is nobody—and everybody."

—*Warren Moscow* (1967)

❖ ❖ ❖

Govern the people with the utmost caution and leniency, for you have now learned by experience, how too much vehemence may draw upon you the hatred of the people.

—*West India Company directors,*
letter to Peter Stuyvesant (c. 1652)

❖ ❖ ❖

Above 500 ladies of pleasure keep lodgings contiguous within the consecrated liberties of St. Paul's. This part of the city belongs to the church, and has thence obtained the name of the Holy Ground. Here all the prostitutes reside, among whom are many fine well-dressed women, and it is remarkable that they live in much greater cordiality one with another than any nests of that kind do in Britain or Ireland.

—*Patrick M'Robert, a visitor* (1774)

The fire department in New York . . . is a most wonderful thing. As the point of honor is to be first at a fire, the director of the first engine that arrives, becomes director-general for the evening. He is, as it were, the commander-in-chief of an allied army during a battle. . . . When two engines arrive at a fire at the same time, the companies frequently fight for the first place, and then a desperate and bloody battle will rage for a considerable time, while the flames are making an unchecked progress.

—*Alexander Marjoribanks* (1850)

❖ ❖ ❖

Are there laws against Negroes? Are they outside the common law? No; but public prejudice persecutes them more tyrannically than any law. They are denied the omnibuses, are excluded from the churches. That's how these democrats interpret equality, and these Puritans, Christian charity.

—*Ernest Duvergier de Hauranne, French traveler* (1864)

We have brought machinery to a pitch of perfection that, fifty years ago, could not have been imagined; but, in the presence of political corruption, we seem as helpless as idiots. The East River [Brooklyn] bridge is a crowning triumph of mechanical skill; but to get it built a leading citizen of Brooklyn had to carry to New York sixty thousand dollars in a carpet-bag to bribe New York aldermen.

—*Henry George* (1883)

❖ ❖ ❖

Along the waterfronts, in holes of the dock rats, and on the avenues, the young tough finds plenty of kindred spirits. Every corner has its gang not always on the best of terms with the rivals in the next block, but all with a common programme: defiance of law and order, and with a common ambition: to get "pinched": i.e., arrested, so as to pose as heroes before their fellows. The gang is an institution in New York.

—*Jacob Riis* (1890)

In a heathen land the three things that are supposed to be the pillars of moderately decent government are regard for human life, justice, criminal and civil, as far as it lies in man to do justice, and good roads. In this Christian city, they think lightly of the first—their own papers, their own speech, and their own actions prove it; buy and sell the second at a price openly and without shame; and are, apparently, content to do without the third.

—*Rudyard Kipling* (1892)

❖ ❖ ❖

There is more law in the end of a policeman's nightstick than in a decision of the Supreme Court.

—*Police Inspector Alexander S. Williams* (early 1900s)

❖ ❖ ❖

That's what I love about the NYPD. . . . It's more than a job—it's a front row ticket to the best show on Earth.

—*NYPD Detective Ken Robinson*

The Police Commissioner of New York City explains the wave of crime in that city by blaming the newspapers. The newspapers, he says, are constantly printing accounts of robberies and murders, and these accounts simply encourage other criminals to come to New York and do the same.

—*Robert Benchley* (1922)

❖ ❖ ❖

A neighborhood is where, when you go out of it, you get beat up.

—*Murray Kempton* (1963)

❖ ❖ ❖

The assumption of corruption among New York politicians ignores the fact that wrong-doing is human rather than a local phenomenon, and that if New York is an exception in the field, it is because its trend is more in the direction of righteousness.

—*Warren Moscow* (1967)

Chinese deliverymen are one of the most vulnerable species in the urban ecosystem. Homicide is a leading cause of on-the-job deaths; the motive is nearly always robbery. Five New York City Chinese deliverymen were killed between 1998 and 2003 alone, simply for the free food and a handful of cash. None of their killers were even old enough to drink.

—Jennifer 8. Lee

❖ ❖ ❖

A detective who has had a lot of experience on the Mendicant Squad says that slightly more than half the beggars who appear blind or crippled are frauds. He knew of one blinkie who tapped his way around Times Square for years, doing pretty well at begging until he took to supplementing his income by picking pockets at night. When he was caught at it in a bar at Seventh Avenue near Forty-seventh Street, he explained that, being blind, he thought his fingers were in his own pocket.

—Meyer Berger (1983)

Every day, subway riders find themselves inches from people with whom they would not willingly choose to share a long city block. But like schoolchildren in detention, riders form a kind of unspoken bond while forced into each others' company—call it the kinship of the mildly oppressed.

—*Randy Kennedy* (2004))

13

SUBWAY LIVING

New York people will never go into a hole in the ground to ride.

—Russell Sage, on the proposed subway system (c. 1891)

❖ ❖ ❖

The people are growing to like the Subway method of transit, and the growth of their liking, great and measurable as it is, has only begun.

—Edward P. Bryan, vice president of the Interborough Rapid Transit Company (1905)

❖ ❖ ❖

The subway is magnificent as any temple. Mortals of Greece/carved exquisite edifices, but of modest scale, for the select;/mortals of this teeming city bored through rock as hard,/for hundreds of miles, for the daily millions!

—Daniel Evan Weiss (1999)

It was in no sheltered nook/It was by no babbling brook/
When romantic'lly we met./Ah, the scene I can't forget/
We were thrown together in the Subway Express.

—*James O'Dean and Jerome Kern*
("The Subway Express," 1907)

❖ ❖ ❖

He lost her in the subway, down at the City Hall.
He married her that morning. That night he had no bride at all.
Just think of his dilemma. No honeymoon that day.
Oh me, oh my, I could cry. He lost her in the old subway.

—*Ada Jones, quoted by Randy Kennedy* (1907)

❖ ❖ ❖

At Third Avenue they took the elevated . . . it was better
than the theater.

—*William Dean Howells*

July 1921: Subway workers report that they have begun to notice oddly enthusiastic people who ride the subway all day with no particular destination in mind. They refer to these people as "joy riders" or "buffs."

—*Randy Kennedy* (2004)

❖ ❖ ❖

Faces, hats, hands, newspapers, jiggled in the fetid roaring subway car like corn in a popper.

—*John Dos Passos* (1925)

❖ ❖ ❖

If you want to go to Harlem,/Way up to Sugar Hill,/ Where those dancing feet you read of/Are never, never, still,/Then you must take the A train/To go to Sugar Hill/ Way up in Harlem.

—*Billy Strayhorn* ("Take the A Train," 1933)

Grand Central is a fine place to get lost in, for, in addition to being an indefatigably conscientious subway station, it is a proper railway station and a shopping center and hotel into the bargain, and as it is one of the only two real railway stations in Manhattan, it is a big one.

—*Anthony Armstrong Willis* (1932)

❖ ❖ ❖

I was born in an apartment house at Ninety-third Street and Lexington Avenue, about three miles from where I now live. Friends often tell me of their excitement when the train on which they are riding passes from Indiana into Illinois, or back again. I am ashamed to admit that when the Jerome Avenue express rolls into Eighty-sixth Street station I have absolutely no reaction.

—*A. J. Liebling* (1938)

❖ ❖ ❖

Writers who don't take the subway? They must be out of their minds.

—*Lawrence Block* (2006)

Generally speaking, it's not that hard to get from the outer boroughs to Manhattan, but it's exceedingly difficult to get from one borough to another. If you live in the Bronx, you can't get to Queens, unless you go through Manhattan. If you live in Brooklyn, you can't get to the Bronx, except via Manhattan.

—*Robert Fitch* (1993)

❖ ❖ ❖

My first memory of boarding the IRT was of *not* boarding the IRT: my mother getting on at the Simpson Street station in the East Bronx while I daydreamed on the platform. As the doors slid shut between us, she took her seat and, with what seemed an eerie calm, regarded me as I frantically slapped my palms on the outside of the windows. I was four years old, and when a faceless Samaritan forced the doors to reopen, I rocketed across the car into her lap, acutely aware that some of the passengers were softly laughing at my oversized relief.

—*Richard Price* (2004)

The thing that depressed me the most about the subway
. . . was the graffiti. When the city was on the verge
of bankruptcy in the early seventies, each time I saw a
graffiti-covered subway car, I felt like crying—the graffiti
seemed to me a realistic symbol that my hometown, if
New York City can be called a hometown, was really
going down the drain.

—*Felix Cuervo*

❖ ❖ ❖

You're standing there in the station, everything is gray and
gloomy, and all of a sudden one of those graffiti trains
slides in and brightens the place like a big bouquet from
Latin America. At first, it seems anarchical—makes you
wonder if the subways are working properly. Then you
get used to it. The city is like a newspaper anyway, so it's
natural to see writing all over the place.

—*Claes Oldenberg* (1974)

They put the system together nearly a hundred years ago. It's been out in winter, in summer, snow, sleet, rain, animals urinating all over it—the two-legged animals, okay? I should look that good at a hundred years.

—*Joe Caracciolo, quoted by Jim Dwyer* (1991)

❖ ❖ ❖

Certain nights, when I was restless and nothing was working out, I'd take the D over the Manhattan Bridge. As the train left the tunnel and began to cross the East River I'd step between the cars. This, for some reason, made me happy. It wasn't really dangerous and the view it afforded of New York was beyond words. A city ablaze, suspended between black sky and river.

—*Junot Diaz* (2000)

❖ ❖ ❖

From the thundering underground—the maze of the New York subways—the world pours into Times Square. Like lost souls emerging from the purgatory of the trains.

—*John Rechy*

We inlanders sometimes imagine we have conquered the subway, but our conquest, upon close examination by a native, usually consists of nothing more than some straight shots on the West Side IRT or some rather clumsy combination put together with the Forty-second Street shuttle.

—*Calvin Trillin*

❖ ❖ ❖

The F train rushes out of Manhattan's Lower East Side, a mighty river coursing diagonally deep into the heart of Brooklyn, then petering out somewhere north of Coney. Its cargo is the raw material of the New Brooklyn, refugees from the exorbitant rents of Manhattan, bringing fresh vitality to the peeling warehouses of Dumbo and the old oyster beds of the Gowanus Canal. Each stop is a filter that skims off distinct types.

—*Danny Gregory* (2004)

A subway crush is simply someone you most likely will never talk to or even meet, but will stare at adoringly from afar. It's a crush in the simplest, most intense sense of the word. During the limited span of your ride, you can imagine any future you want with this person. She or he may not even be your type, but you find yourself becoming temporarily infatuated.

—*Jason Gordon* (2004)

❖ ❖ ❖

They put a nut in every car.

—*Bill Cosby* (1963)

❖ ❖ ❖

Learn to stand in the train without holding on to a strap. Keep your hands down and keep a long sharp pin in your pocket. If you feel a man's hand on you, stick it good with the pin.

—*Betty Smith* (1943)

My friends and my neighbors, they ask me for money
I'm broker than they are, I laugh 'cause it's funny
Oh who do they think I am, some damned Easter bunny?
I'm only a subway musician.

—Brian Homa, subway musician,
quoted by Randy Kennedy (2004)

❖ ❖ ❖

The novelist Paul Theroux once spent a week riding the system from end to end, and imparted his most important survival technique, given to him by a friend: "You have to look as if you're the one with the meat cleaver."

—Randy Kennedy (2004)

❖ ❖ ❖

I can't even enjoy a blade of grass unless I know there's a subway handy.

—Frank O'Hara

n ew York is certainly altogether the most bustling, cheerful, lifeful, restless city I have yet seen in the United States. Nothing and nobody seem to stand still for half a moment in New York.

—*Lady Emmeline Stuart-Wortley* (1850)

14

By Foot, By Wheel,
By Air, By Water

The streets of New York are not to be perambulated
with impunity by either the lame, or the blind, or the
exquisitely sensitive in their olfactory nerves.

—*John M. Duncan, a Scottish visitor* (1823)

❖ ❖ ❖

Circumambulate the city of a dreamy Sabbath afternoon.
Go from Corlears Hook to Coenties Slip, and from
thence, by White-hall, northward. What do you see?—
Posted like silent sentinels all around the town, stand
thousands upon thousands of mortal men fixed in ocean
reveries.

—*Herman Melville* (1851)

❖ ❖ ❖

[Manhattan] has value only along its spinal column; the
borders are slums. On foot, you can walk across town in
twenty minutes and see that spectacle of contrasts.

—*Le Corbusier* (1936)

You can never get lost in New York, as long as you keep moving, but you can get stuck sometimes. It depends on your stamina more than your sense of direction.

—*Edward Conlon*

❖ ❖ ❖

I have at last, after several months' experience, made up my mind that it is a splendid desert—a domed and steepled solitude, where the stranger is lonely in the midst of a million of his race. A man walks his tedious miles through the same interminable street every day, elbowing his way through a buzzing multitude of men, yet never seeing a familiar face, and never seeing a strange one the second time.

—*Mark Twain* (1867)

Before 1895 the streets were almost universally in a filthy state. In wet weather they were covered with slime, and in dry weather the air was filled with dust. Artificial, sprinkling in summer converted the dust into mud, and the drying winds changed the mud to powder . . . It was not always possible to see the pavement because of the dirt that covered it.

—*Colonel George Waring* (1897)

❖ ❖ ❖

She has become a wicked and wild bitch in her old age . . . but there is still no sensation in the world quite like walking her sidewalks. Great surges of energy sweep all around you, the air fizzes like champagne, while always there is a nervous edge of fear and whispered distant promises of sudden violence.

—*Tom Davies* (1979)

---❖---

Cut off as I am, it is inevitable that I should sometimes feel like a shadow walking in a shadowy world. When this happens I ask to be taken to New York City. Always I return home weary but I have the comforting certainty that mankind is real and I myself am not a dream.

—*Helen Keller* (1968)

❖ ❖ ❖

Within a few days you will have adopted the New York walk. Rapidly, skillfully, you negotiate the jammed sidewalks at twice your hometown pace; triumphant as an athlete at the end of a well-played game, you conquer the congestion.

—*Michele Landsberg* (1989)

❖ ❖ ❖

My mother is an urban peasant and I am my mother's daughter. The city is our natural element. We each have daily adventures with bus drivers, bag ladies, ticket takers, and street crazies. Walking brings out the best in us.

—*Vivian Gornick* (1987)

❖

You learn what the city is when you come back after a vacation. It's a shock. You have to tighten your reflexes, tighten your act. You have to regalvanize yourself into the city's tempo. You've got to rally, as one of my bartenders used to say.

—*Bradley Cunningham* (2006)

❖ ❖ ❖

If I'm not in the mood to bump into people and just be around them, I would go outside the crowds. I can find a street that has nobody on it. It could be in the middle of the biggest rush hour ever and there's one street in New York City that has nobody on it.

—*Maggie Nesciur* (2009)

So my grandmother was thirteen when she made that three-month journey [from Russia] of train and boats and steerage, arriving here in 1905. She lived two blocks from where I grew up in East Flatbush, and when I was eight, she was always terrified I would be crossing the intersection of Remsen Avenue, Linden Boulevard, and Kings Highway by myself. I used to tell her, "You crossed half the world by yourself when you were my age." She'd say, "Yeah, but there was less traffic."

—*Ira Glasser* (2008)

❖ ❖ ❖

I was born in the city and always assumed I'd grow old here. Little did I know I'd experience a preview of what it's like to be a frail New Yorker after my arthroscopic surgery, when I had to navigate these fast-paced streets with a swollen knee, a limp, and a cane.

—*Candy Schulman* (2009)

Domesticated animals will cease to be domesticated within the limits of towns. Indeed, I believe that twenty years will not elapse before the horse will be unknown in New York, and that automobile carriages and trucks will entirely supplant the vehicles of today. Heavens! What a relief this will be to the Department of Street Cleaning.

—*Colonel George Waring* (1897)

❖ ❖ ❖

There is one thing very sure—I can't keep my temper in New York. The cars and carriages always come along and get in the way just as I want to cross a street, and if there is any thing that can make a man soar into flights of sublimity in the matter of profanity, it is that thing.

—*Mark Twain* (1867)

❖ ❖ ❖

The motorist whirs through the intersecting streets and round the corners, bent on suicide or homicide.

—*William Dean Howells* (1908)

I have driven rapidly in a fast car, clinging to my hat and my hair against the New York wind, from one end of Fifth Avenue to the other. . . . I have been positively intoxicated.

—Arnold Bennett (1911)

❖ ❖ ❖

A car is useless in New York, essential everywhere else. The same with good manners.

—Mignon McLaughlin

❖ ❖ ❖

I went to the Lower East Side one Sunday morning to take a look at the city's experiment of turning Orchard Street into a "mall" on Sunday by forbidding automobile traffic from Delancey to Houston. I found that the absence of cars did make Orchard Street much less crowded and chaotic, which would have been all to the good except that Orchard Street is *supposed* to be crowded and chaotic.

—Calvin Trillin (1994)

In the summer in New York, the streets turn into rivers of molten tar, like a Venice from hell, with crazed cabdrivers careening like possessed gondoliers.

—*David McGlynn*

❖ ❖ ❖

Caught on a side street
in heavy traffic, I said
to the cabbie, I should
have walked. He replied,
I should have been a doctor.

—*Harvey Shapiro* ("New York Notes," 2001)

❖ ❖ ❖

One thing you notice as you approach New York City, is that there are almost no signs saying "Manhattan." Instead the traveler is introduced to such notions as "Moshulu" and "Major Deegan."

—*Nick Paumgarten*

❖

Seventy years ago today, New York City's Holland Tunnel was opened to traffic. And just this afternoon, those first six cars made it through into New Jersey.

—*Gabe Abelson* (1997)

❖ ❖ ❖

The traffic on Canal Street never stops. It is a high-energy current jumping constantly between the poles of Brooklyn and New Jersey. It hates to have its flow pinched in the density of Manhattan, hates to stop at intersections. Along Canal Street, it moans and screams. Worn brake shoes of semi trucks go "Ooohhhh noohhhh" at stoplights, and the sound echoes in the canyons of the warehouses and Chinatown tenements.

—*Ian Frazier* (1990)

There is nothing relaxed about the summer city. New York's noise is louder, New York's toughness is brasher. New York's velocity is speedier. Everything—stores, offices, schedules, vacations, traffic—demands full steam ahead; no one can say that the livin' is easy.

—*Cynthia Ozick* (2000)

❖ ❖ ❖

With all due respect to LSD, nothing could be more mind-expanding than a trip Helen [Hayes] and I took with a load of New York City garbage. We were on a tugboat that was towing a fleet of sanitation barges down the Harbor. They were piled high with plastic bags full of trash, their brilliant colors glittering in the autumn sunshine: turquoise, aquamarine, and icy white, as if they were cargoes from a world of fantasy.

—*Anita Loos* (1972)

Personally, I've always favored New York 'cause this is one city where you don't have to ride in the back of the bus. Not that they're liberal—it's just that in New York, nobody moves to the back of the bus.

—*Dick Gregory* (1962)

❖ ❖ ❖

Noise and human hurry and a vastness of means and collective result, rather than any vastness of achievement, is the pervading quality of New York. The great thing is the mechanical thing, the unintentional thing which is speeding up all these people.

—*H. G. Wells* (1906)

❖ ❖ ❖

As the ship glided up the river, the city burst thunderously upon us in the early dusk. . . . A band started to play on deck, but the majesty of the city made the march trivial and tinkling. From that moment I knew that New York, however often I might leave it, was home.

—*F. Scott Fitzgerald*

The time will come when New York will be built up, when all the grading and filling will be done, and when the picturesquely-varied, rocky formations of the Island will have been converted into formations for rows of monotonous straight streets, and piles of erect buildings. There will be no suggestion left of its present varied surface, with the single exception of a few acres contained in the [Central] Park.

—*Frederick Law Olmsted* (1858)

15
THE NATURAL WORLD

❖

I always think it a pity that greater favor is not given to the natural hills and slopes of the ground on the upper part of Manhattan Island. Our perpetual dead flat, and streets cutting each other at right angles, are certainly the last things in the world consistent with beauty of situation.

—*Walt Whitman* (1849)

❖ ❖ ❖

[Set] off . . . to explore the Central Park, which will be a feature of the city within five years and a lovely place in A.D. 1900 when its trees will have acquired dignity and appreciable diameters. Perhaps the city itself will perish before then, by growing too big to live under faulty institutions corruptly administered.

—*George Templeton Strong* (1859)

❖

The [Central] Park is recent, hardly finished, yet it already swarms each evening with beaux and carriages, especially those remarkable American vehicles whose slender wheels resemble filigreed jewelry, and which run along like big spiders with long legs.

—*Ernest Duvergier de Hauranne,*
French traveler (1864)

❖ ❖ ❖

No one who has closely observed the conduct of the people who visit the Park, can doubt that it exercises a distinctly harmonizing and refining influence upon the most unfortunate and most lawless classes of the city—an influence favorable to courtesy, self-control, and temperance.

—*Frederick Law Olmsted* (1870)

The Central Park, so called from being a magnificent expanse of wilderness in the center of nothing, is ill-kept and ragged, and at night is unsafe for either sex.

—*Lepel Griffin* (1884)

❖ ❖ ❖

The elders of passing generations have seem armies of geese on their southern migration, and flocks of ducks hanging over the Harlem flats, so thick as to cast their shadows on the plain like obscuring clouds.

—*James Grant Wilson* (c. 1890)

❖ ❖ ❖

Any fool can stand upon a hill in the country and be aware that grass is up and trees have begun to bud; but in the city spring is served à la carte rather than in heaping portions. . . . I sometimes think that never blooms a tulip quite so red as that which shows its head in a Park Avenue flower bed between the traffic.

—*Heywood Broun*

Few people would believe that there are still more trees in New York than buildings, but there are more than a million of them, nearly all belonging to the city. There'd be more if it were not for leaky gas mains and reckless motorists, chief causes in Manhattan at least of tree mortality.

—*New York Panorama* (1938)

❖ ❖ ❖

If you really want to study trees, Central Park is hard to beat. The park is vast, so big you can get lost in it, so big they say that you can see it from a spaceship. . . . With fifty-eight miles of meandering pathways and 843 acres, it's a park a king would be proud of. It has hills, meadows, forests, groves, lakes, ponds, streams, and waterfalls. It even has a castle.

—*Sam Swope* (2004)

If a Park Ranger in Yellowstone is responsible for the preservation and safety of that landscape, Central Forestry is no less responsible for the preservation and safety of New York City's street-tree forest. For my job, and my pleasure, I think about New York City's plants.

—*Bram Gunther* (2009)

❖ ❖ ❖

I like to walk around Manhattan, catching glimpses of its wild life, the pigeons and cats and girls.

—*Rex T. Stout* (1956)

❖ ❖ ❖

Some days nice weather is as annoying as a fire drill; it requires you to evacuate the premises but gives you no particular place to be. After much circling around I always seem to touch down at the park. For one thing, it's about the only place you can sit.

—*Said Shirazi* (2009)

The outdoors is what you have to pass through to get from your apartment to a taxicab.

—*Fran Lebowitz*

❖ ❖ ❖

In New York City, the best places to look for wild flowers are old cemeteries and old churchyards.

—*Joseph Mitchell* (1956)

❖ ❖ ❖

I often feel drawn to the Hudson River, and I have spent a lot of time through the years poking around the part of it that flows past the city. I never get tired of looking at it; it hypnotizes me. I like to look at it in midsummer, when it is warm and dirty and drowsy, and I like to look at it in January, when it is carrying ice.

—*Joseph Mitchell* (1959)

Manhattan has only two seasons: shiver and swelter. Digging ourselves out from a crippling crust of snow, as we did many times this winter, we long for the bright, balmy days of summer, conveniently forgetting about the *h* word. It's not the heat, as they say, it's the humidity. But heat, humidity, whatever, it always seems worse in the city than anywhere else.

—*Lee Stringer* (1985)

❖ ❖ ❖

In the city, the wind is like a giant nudge, a full-body wink, an in-your-face and in-your-hair reminder that you live outdoors, that steam and electricity and water from faraway reservoirs and sewage aren't the only things that course through the city every day.

—*Robert Sullivan* (2008)

The rats of New York are quicker-witted than those on farms, and they can outthink any man who has not made a study of their habits. Even so, they spend most of their lives in a state of extreme anxiety, the black rats dreading the brown and both species dreading human beings.

—*Joseph Mitchell* (1944)

❖ ❖ ❖

I always say that if you killed every rat in New York City, you would have created new housing for sixty million rats.

—*Dan Markowski* (2004)

❖ ❖ ❖

Striped bass are in many respects the perfect New York fish. They go well with the look of downtown. They are, for starters, pinstriped; the lines along their sides are black fading to light cobalt blue at the edges. The dime-sized silver scales look newly minted, and there is an urban glint to the eye and a mobility to the wide predator jaw.

—*Ian Frazier* (1994)

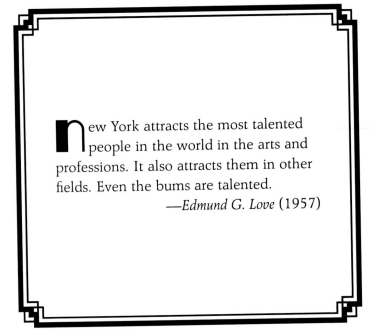

new York attracts the most talented people in the world in the arts and professions. It also attracts them in other fields. Even the bums are talented.

—*Edmund G. Love* (1957)

Down And Hiding Out

No other road in North America has been disreputable for so many decades.

—*Richard Beard, describing the Bowery*
(cited by Jennifer Toth, 1993)

❖ ❖ ❖

See, the Bowery is a place but it's also a state of mind. People feel worthless. They don't give a damn anymore. They're in the Bowery state of mind.

—*Don Stern* (1999)

❖ ❖ ❖

This is an "eat it and beat it" hotel—people are supposed to come and stay for a day or two and get out. But for some reason, people like to stay—for *years*. We don't have any amenities here at all—no soap, no towels, no TVs, no maid service. The only thing you get is a light-bulb and a locker. The Waldorf-Astoria we're not. But it beats living in the streets.

—*Nathan Smith* (1999)

As far as I was concerned, living on the streets was not an insurmountable inconvenience. There were some rough days, before I learned the ins and outs of soup kitchens and such. But once I hooked into picking up cans at a nickel a pop, I couldn't even be bothered with that cattle-call ordeal. And what a pleasure it was to sleep rent- and worry-free under the stars of Central Park.

—Lee Stringer (1985)

❖ ❖ ❖

New York has more hermits than will be found in all the forests, mountains and deserts of the United States.

—Simeon Strunsky (1944)

❖ ❖ ❖

When I was living in New York and didn't have a penny to my name, I would walk around the streets and occasionally I would see an alcove . . . And I'd think . . . that'll be a good spot for me when I'm homeless.

—Larry David

Manhattan Island, at its center, inspires utterly baseless optimism—even in me, even in drunks sleeping in a doorway.

—*Kurt Vonnegut*

❖ ❖ ❖

New York is a place where the rich walk, the poor drive Cadillacs, and beggars die of malnutrition with thousands of dollars hidden in their mattresses.

—*Duke Ellington*

❖ ❖ ❖

On the Bowery, cheap movies rank just below cheap alcohol as an escape, and most bums are movie fans.

—*Joseph Mitchell* (1940)

❖ ❖ ❖

In New York City there are three centers for people living on the street: Central Park, Grand Central Terminal, and Central Booking.

—*Lee Stringer* (1985)

If I were a millionaire instead of homeless, I would
build a hospital with a clear roof, so that every woman
becoming a mother, creating a being which in my eyes
is an angel, would have a window to see the sky. Then it
would be an actual fact everyone was born under the sun,
moon and shining stars.

—*Muhammad Siagha* (2004)

❖ ❖ ❖

"Can you spare a dollar for an out-of-work poet?". . .

"What's up?" I asked, riffling through my pockets for a
spare buck. "You only used to ask for quarters."

"Sure," he said without batting an eye, "but I'm writing
much better stuff now."

—*Lee Stringer* (1985)

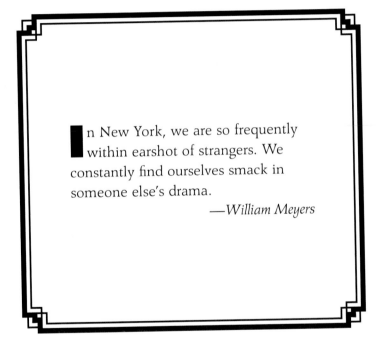

In New York, we are so frequently within earshot of strangers. We constantly find ourselves smack in someone else's drama.

—*William Meyers*

17
Spoken Like a Native

He speaks English with the flawless imperfection of a
New Yorker.

—*Gilbert Millstein*

❖ ❖ ❖

A person who speaks good English in New York sounds
like a foreigner.

—*Jackie Mason*

❖ ❖ ❖

Basically, New Yorkerese is the common speech of early
nineteenth century Cork, transplanted during the mass
immigration of the South Irish a hundred years ago. . . . It
is a jargon, whose principal characteristics appears in the
pronunciation of *th*, as exemplified in *dis, dat, den, dey*.

—*A. J. Liebling* (1938)

To start with, there's the alien accent. "Tree" is the number between two and four. "Jeintz" is the name of the New York professional football team. A "fit" is a bottle measuring seven ounces less than a quart. This exotic tongue has no relationship to any of the approved languages of the United Nations, and is only slightly less difficult to master than Urdu.

—*Fletcher Knebel*

❖ ❖ ❖

Gotham is a verbal city; people are always talking. And they do not make the usual separations between public and private conversation. . . . Every visitor to New York can remember being engaged in a conversation while walking down the street and suddenly being given advice or comment by the stranger walking past him or her.

—*Kenneth T. Jackson and David S. Dunbar* (2002)

New York is a city of people acting out (to use the jargon), folks talking loud to no one or to everyone at once on the IRT—thanking you for your generosity before it's offered, biting your pant leg with their maladies and tales of hard luck. New York is a city of menacing bargains struck by strangers, who ask charity in return for not mugging you or robbing you blind.

—*Guy Trebay* (1994)

❖ ❖ ❖

"Sir," said Samuel Johnson, "when a man is tired of London, he is tired of life."

I don't completely agree with him. Sometimes it really is nice to get out of town. But I know what he meant. Of all contemporary American cities, New York is the closest to Johnson's 18th-century London. It's got the crowding. The variety. The taverns. The huge gap between rich and poor.

—*Elizabeth Gold* (2004)

New Yorkers panic if anything about the Midwest comes into conversation, because one, they don't know anything about it and, two, they're not absolutely sure where it is.

—*Garrison Keillor*

❖ ❖ ❖

In my job I bring a little creativity. I didn't want signs that said WELCOME TO BROOKLYN. That's not Brooklyn. Brooklyn has an edge. We're a bunch of meshuggeners. We are, and I'm proud of that. And I like that. I wanted the signs to reflect what we are. One of them is HOW SWEET IT IS! If you remember, Ralph Kramden [played by Bushwick's Jackie Gleason on *The Honeymooners*] was a Brooklyn bus driver.

—*Brooklyn Borough President Marty Markowitz* (2008)

❖ ❖ ❖

Fuggeddabouddit. Fuggedda. Fugget.
I already Fuggot.

—*Jonathan Lethem* (2008)

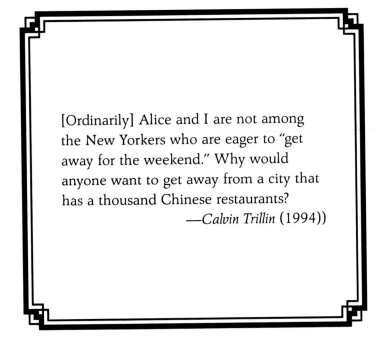

[Ordinarily] Alice and I are not among
the New Yorkers who are eager to "get
away for the weekend." Why would
anyone want to get away from a city that
has a thousand Chinese restaurants?
—*Calvin Trillin* (1994))

18

A Taste of New York

I know of no place where food of every kind is cheaper or more abundant; meat, pork, ham, mutton, butter, cheese, flour, fish, and oysters, all combine to render living wholesome and reasonable; thus everybody lives in comfort, everyone is nurtured on good food, the poorest laborer not excepted.

—*Jean de Crevecoeur* (1772)

❖ ❖ ❖

Hot corn! Hot corn!
Here's your lily white corn.
All you that's got money—
Poor me that's got none—
Come buy my lily hot corn
And let me go home.

—*Song of the Hot Corn*
girls in Five Points,
Manhattan (c. 1830s)

❖

New York abounds beyond all other places in the universe, not excepting Paris, in consummate institutions for cultivating the noble science of gastronomy.

—*James Kirke Paulding* (1828)

❖ ❖ ❖

Everything is done differently in New York from anywhere else, but in eating the difference is more striking than in any other branch of human economy. . . . A regular down-towner surveys the kitchen with his nose as he comes up-stairs—selects his dish by intuition, and swallows it by steam and the electro-galvanic battery. As to digesting it, that is none of his business.

—*George Foster* (1849)

❖ ❖ ❖

Here's clams, here's clams, here's clams today/They late came from Rockaway;/They're good to roast, they're good to fry,/They're good to make a clam pot pie./Here they go!

—*Song of the street vendors* (c. 1850)

The first thing you learned as a little kid was, "There is no egg in egg cream." I wanted to know, "Why do they call it an egg cream?"

"You ask too many questions. Just drink it."

The secret of the egg cream is the chocolate syrup, the glass being chilled appropriately, a chilled spoon, a long spoon, and the seltzer being *spritzed* in at the right level, and then naturally the wrist action where you're beating the chocolate syrup and the seltzer to get that fizz.

—*Curtis Sliwa* (2008)

❖ ❖ ❖

I hope to paint something that will ruin the appetite of every son of a bitch who ever eats in that room [at the Four Seasons].

—*Mark Rothko*

❖ ❖ ❖

Manhattan is a narrow island off the coast of New Jersey devoted to the pursuit of lunch.

—*Raymond Sokolov* (1984)

Chinese restaurants became so common in New York that in 1952 a prominent German restaurant finally caved in and restored to its name the umlaut that had been removed during World War I. Lüchow's owner had gotten tired of tourists coming in and ordering chop suey and egg rolls.

—*Jennifer 8. Lee*

❖ ❖ ❖

New York is where you can get the best cheap meal and the lousiest expensive meal in the country.

—*Robert Weaver* (1992)

❖ ❖ ❖

I grew up during the 1980s on the Upper West Side of Manhattan, where Broadway is sometimes called Szechuan Alley for the density of Chinese restaurants.

—*Jennifer 8. Lee* (2008)

You paid fifteen cents for corned beef and cabbage and twenty-five cents for a turkey dinner. While you ate you felt your pockets frequently to keep them from being picked. In winter you put you overcoat on the back of your chair so that it would not be stolen.

—*Julius Keller, on the "hash-houses"* (c. 1880)

❖ ❖ ❖

The metropolitan education of an intelligent visitor, foreign or American, was incomplete until he had partaken, on a major or minor scale, of the creation of the culinary world, fare in which the delicacies of every zone, from the caviare of Archangel to the "polenta" of Naples, the "allia podrida" of Madrid, the Bouillabaisse of Marseilles, the Casuela of Santiago Chili.

—*Sam Ward (late nineteenth century)*

❖ ❖ ❖

New Yorkers only want to go to places where they can't get a table.

—*Restaurateur* (1909)

Said the Technocrat/To the Plutocrat/To the Autocrat/And the Democrat—/Let's all go eat at the Automat!

—*The Sun* (1933)

❖ ❖ ❖

The New York steak dinner, or "beefsteak," is a form of gluttony as stylized and regional as the riverbank fish fry, the hot-rock clambake, or the Texas barbecue. Some old chefs believe it had its origin sixty or seventy years ago, when butchers from the slaughterhouses on the East River would sneak choice loin cuts into the kitchens of nearby saloons, grill them over charcoal, and feast on them during their Saturday-night sprees.

—*Joseph Mitchell* (1939)

❖ ❖ ❖

Fleur de Sel was perfect, a small romantic restaurant with an expert, impassioned chef in charge. In nearly any other American city, a restaurant of this quality would immediately jump to the top-ten list. . . . In New York, it was simply one of many.

—*William Grimes* (2009)

I went up the steps and out into the bright September sunlight. Harlem! I stood there, dropped my bags, took a deep breath and felt happy again.

—*Langston Hughes* (1940)

9

HOME TO HARLEM

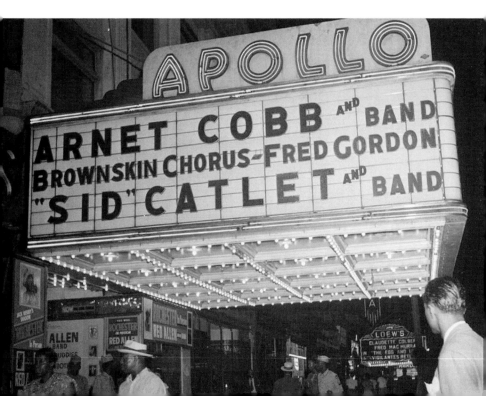

Melting pot Harlem—Harlem of honey and chocolate and caramel and rum and vinegar and lemon and lime and gall. Dusky dream Harlem rumbling into a nightmare tunnel where the subway from the Bronx keeps right on downtown.

—Langston Hughes (1963)

❖ ❖ ❖

New York is the greatest city in the world—especially for my people. Where else, in this grand and glorious land of ours, can I get on a subway, sit in any part of the train I please, get off at any station above 110th Street, and know I'll be welcome?

—Dick Gregory (1962)

Oh, to be in Harlem again after two years away. The deep-dyed color, the thickness, the closeness of it. The noises of Harlem. The sugared laughter. The honey-talk on its streets. And all night long ragtime "blues" playing somewhere . . . singing somewhere, dancing somewhere! Oh, the contagious fever of Harlem. Burning everywhere in dark-eyed Harlem.

—*Claude McKay* (1928)

❖ ❖ ❖

[Thousands] of whites came to Harlem night after night, thinking the Negroes loved to have them there, and firmly believing that all Harlemites left their houses at sundown to sing and dance in cabarets, because most of the whites saw nothing but the cabarets, not the houses.

—*Langston Hughes* (1940)

❖ ❖ ❖

"Dawn never was as pretty in the country as it is sneaking over Lenox Avenue."

—*Langston Hughes's character Jesse B. Simple* (1961)

The "New" in New York is real; like a giant machine, the city creates the newest songs, books, fashions, ideas, slang, monsters, and master-minds that will be tomorrow's news in Halifax or Hong Kong. The newness is a constant stimulant, an addictive drug. Banished to anywhere else, New Yorkers feel deprived, diminished by not being part of the newest and latest.

—*Michele Landsberg* (1989)

20

Bright Lights, Fame, and Fashion

We all know that the theatre and every play that comes to Broadway have within themselves, like the human being, the seed of self-destruction and the certainty of death. The thing is to see how long the theatre, the play, and the human being can last in spite of themselves. The biggest problem of all three is to preserve honorable laughter in a comedy.

—*James Thurber* (1960)

❖ ❖ ❖

For years New York has shouldered the burden of amusing the rest of the country, which appears to be rather dull. The city has even established a *succursale* or bargain basement in California, where retired New Yorkers manufacture a diluted species of dramatics not good enough for New York consumption but fine for the regions without a flesh theatre of their own.

—*A. J. Liebling* (1938)

Broadway is a lady of the evening. In the sunlight she looks like a suddenly awakened chorus girl who went to bed with her make-up on. Her buildings, covered with the unlighted framework of a thousand electric signs, look like a set-piece of fireworks after the fireworks have gone off.

—*C. V. R. Thompson* (1939)

❖ ❖ ❖

New Yorkers rush by the day to save time they will waste at night.

—*Evan Esar* (1968)

❖ ❖ ❖

[The] New Yorker enjoyed his span of being to the full stretch of the tether, his violent exertions during the day counteracting the effects of his nocturnal relaxations, besides giving him a relish to return to them. Certainly few men throughout the Union worked harder for enjoyment.

—*John Bernard*

It is the city of the Good Time, and the Good Time there is so sacred that you may be excused anything you do in searching for it.

—*Ford Madox Ford* (1927)

❖ ❖ ❖

New York City, the incomparable, the brilliant star city of cities, the forty-ninth state, a law unto itself, the Cyclopedian paradox, the inferno with no out-of-bounds, the supreme expression of both miseries and the splendors of contemporary civilization, the Macedonia of the United States. It meets the most severe test that may be applied to definition of metropolis—it stays up all night. But also it becomes a small town when it rains.

—*John Gunther* (1947)

With the advent of night a fantastic city all of fire
suddenly rises from the ocean into the sky. . . . Fabulous
beyond conceiving, ineffably beautiful, is this fiery
scintillation.

—Maxim Gorky (c. 1906)

❖ ❖ ❖

A lost city, hungry for destruction, aching for destruction,
the entire population in a fuss and a fret, a twit and a
twitter, a squit and a squat, a hip and a hop, a snig and a
snaggle, a spism and a spasm, a sweat and a swivet. Can't
wait for night to fall, can't wait for day to break. Even the
church bells sound jangly in New York City; they ring
them too fast.

—Reverend James Jefferson Davis Hall,
quoted by Joseph Mitchell (1943)

If it were not for the peculiar manner of walking, which distinguishes all American women, Broadway might be taken for a French street, where it was the fashion for very smart ladies to promenade. The dress is entirely French; not an article (except perhaps the cotton stockings) must be English, on pain of being stigmatized as out of the fashion.

—*Frances Trollope* (1831)

❖ ❖ ❖

One of the first things that strikes the stranger in New York is the extreme smartness of the women. One rarely comes across a really badly dressed woman in any rank of life. . . . Her Parisian sister, to whom I suppose she would herself admit that she was occasionally indebted for ideas, is not her superior in this respect.

—*Philip Burne-Jones* (1904)

The French will not be happy with what I have to say, but I happen to know that French designers come to New York for inspiration. They go to Central Park, Greenwich Village, and to private parties and then they depart from New York with a portfolio full of ideas. One hippie in the Village can inspire a whole new trend.

—*Raymundo de Larrain*

❖ ❖ ❖

When I first saw New York I was twenty, and it was summertime, and I got off a DC-7 at the old Idlewild temporary terminal in a new dress which had seemed very smart in Sacramento but seemed less smart already.

—*Joan Didion* (1968)

It is a perfect bazaar; not only is there a brilliant display in the windows of everything good to look at, from exotic flowers to encaustic tiles, and everything one can possibly wear, from Paris imported bonnets to pink-satin boots, but the sidewalk is fringed with open-air stalls, heaped high with pretty things, most of them absurdly cheap.

—*Iza Duffus Hardy* (1881)

❖ ❖ ❖

New York is pre-eminently a city of good food, good theaters, fine horses and pretty women.

—*E. Catherine Bates* (1886)

❖ ❖ ❖

There are only about four hundred people in fashionable New York society. If you go outside the number you strike people who are either not at ease in a ballroom or else make other people not at ease.

—*Ward McAllister* (c. 1880s)

There is a very gay, insouciant, and enormously expensive social life in New York, but relatively few names swim to the surface of its whirlpool and those that do are forever changing.
—*Ford Madox Ford* (1927)

❖ ❖ ❖

Like many natural beauties, New York is effortlessly photogenic. It has fabulous bones and hardly any bad angles. It looks good in anything: rain, sunshine, blizzards. Its personality comes through in flashes: antic, sloppy, noble, rude. Its bad days are more exciting than good days anywhere else. And its good days are the best, period.
—*Holland Cotter* (2002)

❖ ❖ ❖

Am sorry my mother is going to grieve,/But I cannot help, I am bound to leave./I got the money, I got the talk,/And the fancy walk just to suit New York.
—*Calypso singer "The Caresser,"*
quoted by Joseph Mitchell (1939)

mass hysteria is a terrible force, yet New Yorkers seem always to escape it by some tiny margin: they sit in stalled subways without claustrophobia, they extricate themselves from panic situations by some lucky wisecrack, they meet confusion and congestion with patience and grit—a sort of perpetual muddling through.

—*E. B. White* (1949)

21
WHEN DISASTER STRIKES

This is a nice town to call itself a center of civilization!
—*George Templeton Strong* (1863)

❖ ❖ ❖

No business was done today. Most shops are closed and draped with black and white muslin. Broadway is clad in "weepers" from Wall Street to Union Square.
—*George Templeton Strong, on the day President Lincoln was assassinated* (April 15, 1865)

❖ ❖ ❖

Outside were thousands of Wall Street refugees walking north. It looked like the city was being evacuated on foot. It looked like a pilgrimage. It looked like a crusade.
—*Bryan Charles* ("The Numbers," 2002)

I was working at my job in the World Financial Center, just across the street from the two seemingly constant World Trade Center towers when the first plane hit. Feeling and hearing the force of the impact, my co-workers and I initially thought the first plane was a freak accident. . . . But then, incredulously looking out the window at the damage and carnage the first plane had inflicted, I saw the second plane abruptly come into my right field of vision and deliberately, with shimmering intention, thunder full-force into Two World Trade. It was so close, so low, so huge and fast, so intent on its target that I swear to you, I swear to you, I felt the vengeance and rage emanating from the plane.

—*Debra Fontaine* ("Witnessing," 2002)

❖ ❖ ❖

[The rescue workers] shouted, "Don't look up! Whatever you do, do not look up! Just keep moving! Do not look up!" But I couldn't help it. I had to see. I turned around and looked up and there were the two towers of the World Trade Center burning. Fire and smoke poured from enormous black holes in both buildings. Real fire, giant lapping tongues of flame. Crisp. Kodachrome. A postcard of someone's nightmare.

—*Bryan Charles* ("The Numbers," 2002)

❖ ❖ ❖

We watched [from the Brooklyn Promenade] thousands of living people, moving like one entity, walking across the Brooklyn Bridge.

It was one of the only beautiful sights on a hideously ugly day. There they all came . . . . their backs literally to death and destruction, as they headed away.

—*Elizabeth Grove* ("This Is Bad," 2002)

--- ❖ ---

New York is still here. We've suffered terrible losses and we will grieve for them, but we will be here, tomorrow and forever.

—*Rudolph Giuliani* (September 11, 2001)

❖ ❖ ❖

From the suburb where I live in New Jersey, you can see the skyline of Manhattan. When it appears through the trees or beyond the edge of a hill, I find myself checking it and checking it again, to see if the World Trade towers still aren't there. What happened to them and to the people in them is unacceptable to the mind, and we must use a lot of effort to get it straight.

—*Ian Frazier* ("The Morning After," 2002)

like the immensities of the borough, the unrolling miles of Eastern Parkway and Ocean Parkway and Linden Boulevard, and the disheveled outlying parks strewn with tree limbs and with shards of glass held together by liquor bottle labels, and the tough bridges—the Williamsburg and the Manhattan—and the gentle Brooklyn Bridge. And I like the way the people talk; some really do have Brooklyn accents, really do say "dese" and "dose."

—*Ian Frazier* (1995)

22

ACROSS THE BROOKLYN BRIDGE

Brooklyn has been increasing with great rapidity of late years. This is owing, partly, to the salubrity of its situation; but chiefly to its vicinity to the business portion of the city; the low price of ferriage (two cents); the facility of access, which can be obtained at all hours, except two in the morning; and, especially, to the high rents of New York.

—*Edgar Allan Poe* (1844)

❖ ❖ ❖

What is it then between us?
What is the count of the scores or hundreds of years between us?
Whatever it is, it avails not—distance avails not, and place avails not,
I too lived, Brooklyn of ample hills was mine.

— *Walt Whitman*
("Crossing Brooklyn Ferry," 1856)

❖

It requires no spirit of prophecy to foretell the union of New York and Brooklyn at no distant day. The river which divides them will soon cease to be a line of separation, and, bestrode by the colossus of commerce, will prove a link which will bind them together.

—*Henry C. Murphy* (1857)

❖ ❖ ❖

Our city is not a jealous city, but then to ask it to build a bridge in order to send its trade to a neighboring city is asking a good deal even from the best of natures.

—*A prominent New Yorker, regarding the proposal
to build the Brooklyn Bridge* (c. 1866)

❖ ❖ ❖

The completed work, when constructed in accordance with my designs, will not only be the greatest bridge in existence, but it will be the greatest engineering work of this continent and of the age.

—*Chief engineer John A. Roebling* (c. 1867)

---❖---

The Brooklyn Bridge has so far helped Brooklyn that our sister city is now sparking us, hoping to be wedded to us, but she must first cleanse herself and put on her best before we will consider her suit.

—*Brooklyn Eagle* (1889),
quoted by Joanna Hershon ("Bridges")

❖ ❖ ❖

A bridge connects New York with Brooklyn, overhanging an arm of the sea. Seen even from afar, this bridge astounds you like one of those architectural nightmares given by Piranesi in his weird etchings. You see great ships passing beneath it, and this indisputable evidence of its height confuses the mind. But walk over it . . . and you will feel that the engineer is the great artist of our epoch.

—*Paul Bourget* (1893)

As a crazed believer/enters/a church,/retreats/into
a monastery cell,/austere and plain;/so I,/in graying
evening/haze,/humbly set foot/on Brooklyn Bridge.
> —*Vladimir Mayakovsky* ("Brooklyn Bridge," 1925)

❖ ❖ ❖

O harp and altar, of the fury fused,
(How could mere toil align thy choiring strings!)
> —*Hart Crane* ("To Brooklyn Bridge," 1930)

❖ ❖ ❖

Walking across the Brooklyn Bridge was like walking into
an enormous spider web.
> —*Mary Cantwell*

❖ ❖ ❖

. . . way out; way in; romantic passageway
first seen by the eye of the mind,
then by the eye. O steel! O stone!
Climactic ornament, a double rainbow.
> —*Marianne Moore* ("Granite and Steel")

I've walked over the Brooklyn Bridge many times, and I've always felt impressed by it. I used to make it my cathedral, the place where I could get close to the Almighty.

—Buckminster Fuller (1971)

❖ ❖ ❖

[The] architecture of the past, massive and protective, meets the architecture of the future, light, aerial, open to sunlight, an architecture of voids rather than solids.

—Lewis Mumford, of the Brooklyn Bridge (2004)

❖ ❖ ❖

Brooklyn's finished record as a city is creditable and indestructible.

—St. Clair McKelway (1897)

❖ ❖ ❖

This is one of the things I loved best about Brooklyn. Everyone is not expected to be exactly like everyone else.

—Carson McCullers (1941)

❖

The genius of Brooklyn has always been its homey
atmosphere; it does not set out to awe or intimidate, like
skyscraper Manhattan—which is perhaps why one hears
so much local alarm at the luxury apartment towers that
have started to sprout up, every two blocks, in those parts
of the borough lying close to Manhattan.

—*Philip Lopate* (2008)

❖ ❖ ❖

New York is Babylon: Brooklyn is the truly Holy City.
New York is the city of envy, office work, and hustle;
Brooklyn is the region of homes and happiness. . . .
There is no hope for New Yorkers, for they glory in their
skyscraping sins; but in Brooklyn there is the wisdom of
the lowly.

—*Christopher Morley* (1917)

❖ ❖ ❖

In Brooklyn everyone was funny.

—*Jackie Gleason*

Typically Miss Manhattan is a tall, liberated young woman with the stride of a man, a pony face, and long stringy hair. She is too self-sufficient, snobbish, and opinionated to be messing about with a Humphrey Bogart character like Brooklyn. But the two seem to magnetize each other; to be truly yin and yang. And in one particular way they are excessively unlike: Manhattan forever runs itself down while Brooklyn is supercharged with pride in Brooklyn.

—*Anita Loos* (1972)

❖ ❖ ❖

Comparing the Brooklyn that I know with Manhattan is like comparing a comfortable and complacent duenna to her more brilliant and neurotic sister.

—*Carson McCullers* (1941)

The Dodgers were my whole life. There was a sense of pride. I always looked at things deeper than my friends did. I said to myself, What are the odds of being born in this world where countless billions of people have been born, lived their lives, and died in abject misery, poverty, and disease, and how lucky can I be to be born in the United States of America *and* in Brooklyn?

—*John Mackie* (2008)

❖ ❖ ❖

[The idea] of walking through Prospect Park to see a rare night game at Ebbets Field—you felt like F. Scott Fitzgerald first seeing the ivory towers of New York. You would walk around the lake on a balmy summer's evening . . . and then you would get to within perhaps two hundred yards of the ballpark, and from the horizon the rim of lights of Ebbets Field would become visible, and you'd keep walking, and all of a sudden the sky would be lit up.

—*Joe Flaherty, reminiscing on the 1940s* (2008)

Brooklyn, New York, has the undefined, hard-to-remember shape of a stain. . . . People in Brooklyn do not describe where they live in terms of north or west or south. They refer instead to their neighborhoods and to the nearest subway lines.

—*Ian Frazier* (1995)

❖ ❖ ❖

It'd take a guy a lifetime to know Brooklyn t'roo and t'roo. An' even den, yuh wouldn't know it all.

—*Thomas Wolfe* (1935)

❖ ❖ ❖

Brooklyn through the scratched window of the elevated train goes on and on, like Chinese boxes, one fitted into the next, only it's laundry lines, little squares of yard, the tops of buildings, smokestacks, houses like gray cards.

—*Gerry Albarelli* (2000)

Most of my relatives from my dad's side of the family came to New York because that's where the jobs were. My mom and daddy came to Brooklyn in 1957. They came to Brooklyn because it was more affordable than Manhattan and less racist than Queens. I'm not saying it wasn't racist. It was *less* racist.

—*Abram Hall* (2008)

❖ ❖ ❖

Brooklyn gives you a backbone, and when you show somebody from Brooklyn an opening, a light, and the person believes it's the right way to go, get out of his or her way. Nothing can stop them.

—*Bruce* ("Cousin Brucie") *Morrow* (2008)

I grew up in amber-waves-of-grain America, more than fifteen hundred miles west of New York City, but it was in Brooklyn that I learned what it meant to live in a small town.

—*Philip Dray* (2008)

❖ ❖ ❖

I am a patriot—of the 14th Ward in Brooklyn [Williamsburg], where I was raised. The rest of the United States doesn't exist for me, except as an idea, or history, or literature.

—*Henry Miller*

❖ ❖ ❖

In Brooklyn, downtownness is, generally speaking, dispersed, spread throughout various neighborhoods, and downtown Brooklyn, possibly as a result, is, on first glance, less spectacular-seeming, more workaday, more middle urban America.

—*Robert Sullivan* (2008)

Coney Island is not a place where the fashionable or aristocratic multitude most do congregate; it is a rather fast, jolly, rollicking place, and serves its purpose well, as the health-breathing lungs of a great city.

—*Mary Duffus Hardy* (1881)

❖ ❖ ❖

If a man is troubled with illusions concerning the female form divine and wishes to be rid of those illusions he should go to Coney Island and closely watch the thousands of women who bathe there every Sunday.

—*Richard K. Fox* (1883)

❖ ❖ ❖

The nighttime air at Coney Island smells like corn dogs and fried clams and a little bit like garbage. It's a good smell once you get used to it, and a good place. . . . For an old man who's kind of curious, but also kind of not interested in talking to anyone, it's perfect.

—*Neal Pollack*

Coney Island, that marvelous city of lath and burlap, should always be approached by sea, as then, and then only, can the beauty of this ephemeral Venice be appreciated. Landward, the trains run through squalid neighborhoods, and past the back of everything. Its best foot is put forward to the sea.

—*Scientific American*

❖ ❖ ❖

A brief word on the Gypsy fortune-tellers, several of whom have set up shop at Coney Island. First of all, it should be made clear that they do not tell fortunes. Fortune-telling is illegal in New York State, except for clergymen and economists.

—*Professor Solomon*

❖ ❖ ❖

[A man] who suffered in a trolley ride what he endured at Coney Island would be committed to a sanitarium for life and would sue the trolley company.

—*John B. Manbeck* (1997)

"Stop moping and go to Brighton Beach," Pavel would tell him. "You would feel right at home." But Sergey never felt at home there. He loathed the gloomy brownstones, the loud store windows, the honking cars, the gray ocean, the cold sand. . . . This was the fake Russia, a parody of Russia, that made the real Russia seem even farther away and hopelessly unattainable.

—*Lara Vapnyar* (2008)

❖ ❖ ❖

Everything Russian on Brighton Beach is too Russian, far more Russian than in real Russia. This is what happens all over Brooklyn. From the Scandinavians of Bay Ridge to the Chinese of Sunset Park, Brooklyn's immigrants go to ridiculous extremes to re-create their homelands only to end up with a vulgar pastiche.

—*Lara Vapnyar* (2003)

My world was my block. When I walked from 95th Street
to 93rd Street, where my grandparents lived, it was scary
and ominous, because there were kids you didn't know.
I used to joke you needed a passport to go to 94th Street.
We're talking about one block. It was scary, because what
if you met some kids you didn't know?

—Ira Glasser (2008)

❖ ❖ ❖

[Bushwick], like virtually all New York neighborhoods, is
very much a historical shell through which great churnings
of people pass: there are practically no old New York
families, practically no New York neighborhoods where
familial lines extend more than a single generation or two.

—Jim Dwyer (1991)

❖ ❖ ❖

Most of us who live in Canarsie came from ghettos. But
once we made it to Canarsie, we finally had a little piece
of the country. It was like we had moved to a little shtetl.

—Anonymous, quoted by Jonathan Rieder (1985)

Canarsie was God's country back then [c. 1930s], because the farther you went east, you would start hitting undeveloped areas, fields and lots, old farms still, and to my grandfather, this was nirvana. He felt like Lewis and Clark of Brooklyn. He said, "I'm going to save my money, and I'm gonna buy a house in Canarsie." People would look at him and say, "Canarsie?"

—*Curtis Sliwa* (2008)

❖ ❖ ❖

Back in those days, the Italians and Irish people didn't refer to their neighborhood by name but by which church you went to. Today the neighborhood is called Park Slope by the nouveau riche. In those days, when someone asked where you came from, you said, "Holy Name," or "Immaculate Heart of Mary," which in Brooklyn was always known as "Our Lady of Perpetual Help." And you never went to Manhattan. Manhattan was always referred to as "the city," and it was always said with a certain dread.

—*Joe Flaherty on the 1940s* (2008)

For years I've been answering the questions, "You live in New York City? Like, right in New York City?" I live in Brooklyn Heights, but this is a distinction meaningful only to those with 100-zip code prefixes.

—*Elizabeth Grove* (2002)

❖ ❖ ❖

Fulton Mall is a stretch of old Brooklyn department stores abandoned in the seventies and recolonized in the eighties and nineties by discount electronics stores, discount shoe stores, discount sneaker stories, discount hat stores, stores that sell discounted goods at a discount.

—*Robert Sullivan* (2008)

❖

I too had crossed the East River in search of affordable housing. After seventeen years in Manhattan, years that included college and graduate school, I had joined the mighty wave of pilgrims with wedding china in their trunks and buns in the oven.

—*Alexandra Styron* (2008)

❖ ❖ ❖

Though borough it may be, Brooklyn it is, Brooklyn it remains and Brooklynites are we!

—*St. Clair McKelway (1897)*

my father's story, in 1948, was Queens, and the best thing about Queens was that it wasn't Brooklyn. It was a stepping stone, a way station: next stop, somewhere else. The only goal my father can remember from that time was to keep going.

—*John Burnham Schwartz* (2008)

23

THE BRONX, QUEENS, AND STATEN ISLAND

---❖---

[The Bronx] . . . a place with a name so remarkable must itself be remarkable.

—*Arnold Bennet* (1911)

❖ ❖ ❖

The Bronx?
No Thonx!

—*Ogden Nash* ("Geographical Reflection," 1931)

❖ ❖ ❖

From 1950 to 1968, we lived on White Plains Road in a housing project in the Williamsbridge section of the Bronx. The el tracks that cast the cobblestones of that endless strip into permanent, grid-patterned shadow also bisected the world at eye level outside our third-floor windows. Yet by dint of the unrelenting lull-roar-lull rhythms out in the street, the trains that ran along those tracks were as subliminally comforting to me as a parental heartbeat.

—*Richard Price* (2004)

The years I spent at P.S. 99 [in the Bronx] continued my development in learning to read and write, and also in learning to curse, intimidate, and fight. I was a fast learner both inside the classroom and out. By the time I reached the sixth grade it was recognized by all the tough boys in school that not only would I fight but I knew *how* to fight.

—*Geoffrey Canada*

❖ ❖ ❖

There is a reason I worry about our children in the summertime. Most of the times I was in serious danger in the South Bronx were during the summer. Our small apartments were like ovens. It was impossible to stay in them during July and August. . . . It was like a street carnival every day. But the evenings belonged to the young men. This was the most exciting time to be out. It could be a quiet night of talk and bragging, or it could be a night that you would never forget.

—*Geoffrey Canada*

Though visible behind me, just across the river, the towers of Manhattan seemed a world away. Queens is different, its buildings only a few stories high, and from the train I had a view both intimate and vast, with fleeting glimpses into windows just across the way and beyond, a panorama of tarred and shingled rooftops, chimneys, antennae, trees, satellite dishes, phone poles, car washes, small factories, and billboards.

—*Sam Swope* (2004)

❖ ❖ ❖

Off and on, I get a thing for walking in Queens. . . . I think what drew me on was the phrase "someplace in Queens." This phrase is often used by people who live in Manhattan to describe a Queens location. They don't say the location is simply "in Queens"; they say it is "someplace in Queens," or "in Queens someplace."

—*Ian Frazier* (1998)

As soon as I was in the noisy chaos underneath the El, I felt like a tourist. I'd never seen a place like this, so foreign yet without a single ethnic identity, not a Chinatown or a Little Italy but Immigrant World . . . Colombian hairdressers, Indian spice shops, Korean wedding stores, Italian bakeries, storefront mosques, Dominican lawyers, Pakistani candy shops, Chinese green markets, Irish pubs, Mexican groceries, Hindu temples, English-language schools, and restaurants of every description.

—*Sam Swope* (2004)

❖ ❖ ❖

You knew you were in Rockaway Beach because all the kids had freckles. No Italian kid had freckles. Maybe a mole. Never a freckle. But all the Irish kids had freckles, and every girl was named Colleen. They had blond hair, blue eyes. You would fall in love with the Colleens.

—*Curtis Sliwa* (2008)

I call up a friend of mine who lives in the outer, unfashionable edges of Queens. "I think I'm going to move," I say. "Good idea," she says. "I couldn't stand living in Manhattan. All those gorgeous young girls, coming in year after year, wave after wave of them. It's like some horrible science fiction movie. You can't stop them. There's always more."

—*Elizabeth Gold* (2005)

❖ ❖ ❖

Staten Island is the Australia of New York City.

—*Dave Hollander*

❖ ❖ ❖

Cuddling geographically with New Jersey, Staten Island was part of New York State only because a sailing captain named Billop circumnavigated it by sloop within twenty-four hours, to win a dare of a royal colonial governor.

—*Warren Moscow* (1967)

At times, out in the [Staten Island] marshes, Mr. Zimmer becomes depressed. The marshes are doomed. The city has begun to dump garbage on them. It has already filled in hundreds of acres with garbage. Eventually, it will fill in the whole area, and then the Department of Parks will undoubtedly build some proper parks out there, and put in some concrete highways and scatter some concrete benches about.

—*Joseph Mitchell* (1951)

❖ ❖ ❖

"I moved out to Staten Island once," an acquaintance told me when I asked if he was not depressed by the tenseness of the city, "but I moved right back again. The silence kept me awake all night."

—*Jan Morris* (1969)

new York is the only city I have ever lived in. I have lived in the country, in the small town, and in New York. It is true I have had apartments in San Francisco, Mexico City, Los Angeles, Paris, and sometimes stayed for months, but that is a very different thing. This is a matter of feeling.

—*John Steinbeck* (1943)

24
I Miss
New York

I miss New York and its fairy-like towers
With Liberty's torch high in the air
I'd give all of California's damn flowers
For the sight of Washington Square.

—*Jessie Tarbox Beals* (1936)

❖ ❖ ❖

I miss New York. I still love how people talk to you on the street—just assault you and tell you what they think of your jacket.

—*Madonna*

❖ ❖ ❖

I never left New York, even for a holiday or family visit at home in Canada, without a long, backward look at the Manhattan skyline and a sense of acute deprivation.

—*Michele Landsberg* (1989)

Every time I go back to Brownsville it is as if I had never been away. From the moment I step off the train at Rockaway Avenue and smell the leak out of the men's room, then the pickles from the stand just below the subway steps, an instant rage comes over me, mixed with dread and some unexpected tenderness.

—*John Burnham Schwartz, quoting his father* (2008)

❖ ❖ ❖

I left New York because, though it nurtured and sustained me like no other place ever has, it also seemed bent on destroying me. It was the pace and the pressure that I fled, the heightened sense of time and movement and energy, the relentlessness of life in a world of pavement, the heavy toll it took on my body and spirit. And yet, like all expatriate New Yorkers, I am drawn back as an ant is drawn back to its hole.

—*Joseph Lieber* (2002)

References

Gerry Albarelli. *Teacha!: Stories from a Yeshiva*. Thetford, Vermont: Glad Day Books. 2000.

Thomas Beller, editor. *Lost and Found: Stories from New York*. New York: Mr. Beller's Neighborhood Books. 2009.

Robert Benchley. *Love Conquers All*. New York. 1922.

Meyer Berger. *Eight Million: Journal of a New York Correspondent*. New York: Columbia University Press. 1983.

Lawrence Block, editor. *Manhattan Noir 2: The Classics*. Akashic Books: New York. 2008.

Edwin G. Burrows and Mike Wallace. *Gotham: A History of New York City to 1898*. New York: Oxford University Press. 1999.

Geoffrey Canada. *Fist Stick Knife Gun: A Personal History of Violence in America*. Boston: Beacon Press, 1995.

Mitchell Duneier. *Sidewalk*. New York: FSG. 1999.

Jim Dwyer. *Subway Lives: 24 Hours in the Life of the New York City Subway*. New York: Crown Publishers. 1991.

Edward Robb Ellis. *The Epic of New York City: A Narrative History*. New York: Basic Books. 2005.

Robert Fitch. *The Assassination of New York*. London: Verso, 1993.

Ian Frazier. *The Fish's Eye: Essays about Angling and the Outdoors*. FSG: New York. 2002.

Ian Frazier. *Gone to New York: Adventures in the City*. FSG: New York. 2005.

Elizabeth Gold. *Brief Intervals of Horrible Sanity: One Season in a Progressive School*. New York: Jeremy Tarcher/Putnam. 2003.

Vivian Gornick. *Fierce Attachments: A Memoir*. Simon & Schuster: New York. 1987

Vivian Gornick. *Approaching Eye Level*. Boston: Beacon Press. 1996.

William Grimes. *Appetite City: A Culinary History of New York*. New York: North Point Press. 2009.

Helen Hayes and Anita Loos. *Twice Over Lightly: New York Then and Now*. New York: Harcourt Brace Jovanovich. 1972.

Langston Hughes. *The Best of Simple*. New York: Hill and Wang. 1961.

Langston Hughes. *The Big Sea*. New York: Alfred A. Knopf. 1940.

Kenneth T. Jackson and David S. Dunbar, editors. *Empire City: New York Through the Centuries*. New York: Columbia University Press. 2002.

Randy Kennedy. *Subway Land: Adventures in the World Beneath New York*. New York: St. Martin's Griffin. 2004.

Michele Landsberg. *"This Is New York, Honey!": A Homage to Manhattan, with Love and Rage*. Toronto: McClelland & Stewart. 1990.

Jennifer 8. Lee. *The Fortune Cookie Chronicles: Adventures in the World of Chinese Food*. New York: Twelve. 2008.

A. J. Liebling. *Back Where I Came From*. San Francisco: North Point Press. 1990.

Philip Lopate, editor. *Writing New York: A Literary Anthology*. New York: Washington Square Press. 2000.

John B. Manbeck. *Brooklyn, Historically Speaking*. Charleston, SC: History Press. 2008.

John B. Manbeck and Lynn H. Butler. *Coney Island Kaleidoscope*. Wilsonville, Oregon: Beautiful America Pub. 1991.

John B. Manbeck and Kenneth T. Jackson, editors. *The Neighborhoods of Brooklyn*. New Haven: Yale University Press. 2004.

Joseph Mitchell. *Up in the Old Hotel and Other Stories*. New York: Vintage Books. 1993.

Jan Morris. *The Great Port: A Passage Through New York*. New York: Oxford University Press. 1985.

Warren Moscow. *What Have You Done for Me Lately?: The Ins and Outs of New York City Politics.* Englewood, New Jersey. 1967.

New York Panorama: A Comprehensive View of the Metropolis, Presented in a Series of Articles Prepared by the Federal Writers' Project of the Works Progress Administration in New York City. New York: Random House. 1938.

Jonathan Rieder. *Canarsie: The Jews and Italians of Brooklyn against Liberalism.* Cambridge, MA: Harvard University Press. 1985.

Harvey Shapiro. *How Charlie Shavers Died and Other Poems.* Wesleyan University Press. 2001.

Russell Shorto. *The Island at the Center of the World: The Epic Story of Dutch Manhattan and the Forgotten Colony That Shaped America.* New York: Vintage Books. 2005.

Professor Solomon. *Coney Island.* Baltimore: Top Hat Press. 1999.

Lee Stringer. *Grand Central Winter: Stories from the Street*. New York: Seven Stories Press. 1998.

George Templeton Strong. *Diary of the Civil War, 1860–1865*. Edited by Allan Nevins and Milton Halsey Thomas. New York: Macmillan, 1952.

Robert Sullivan. *Rats: Observations on the History and Habitat of the City's Most Unwanted Inhabitants*. New York: Bloomsbury. 2004.

Sam Swope. *I Am a Pencil: A Teacher, His Kids, and Their World of Stories*. New York: Henry Holt: New York. 2004.

James Thurber. *Collecting Himself: James Thurber on Writing and Writers, Humor and Himself*. New York: Harper & Row. 1989.

Jennifer Toth. *The Mole People: Life in the Tunnels Beneath New York City*. Chicago: Chicago Review Press. 1993.

Guy Trebay. *In the Place to Be: Guy Trebay's New York*. Philadelphia: Temple University Press. 1994.

Calvin Trillin. *The Tummy Trilogy*. New York: Farrar, Straus and Giroux. 1994.

Leon Trotsky. *My Life*. New York: Pathfinder Press. 1970.

Lara Vapnyar. *Broccoli and Other Tales of Food and Love*. New York: Random House. 2008.

E. B. White. *Here Is New York*. New York: Curtis Publishing. 1949.

❖ ❖ ❖

Illustration credits

Images pages 3, 17, 25, 45, 59, 71, 95, 127, 139, 153, 163, 169, 175, 183, 187, 197, 203, 223, 231 Copyright © 2011 Thinkstock.com.

Images pages 33, 51, 79, 111, and 119 as follows:

Page 33: *Old New York: Yesterday & Today,* Henry Collins Brown. New York: Henry Collins Brown. 1922.

Page 51: *New York Then and Now: 83 Matching Photographic Views from 1864–1938 and from the 1970s,* Edmund V. Gillon, Jr. and Edward B. Watson. New York: Dover Publications, Inc. 1976.

Page 79: *New York in the Nineteenth Century: 321 Engravings from "Harper's Weekly" and Other Contemporary Sources,* John Grafton. New York: Dover Publications, Inc. 1977.

Page 111: Fifth Avenue Old and New 1824–1924, Henry Collins Brown. New York: The Fifth Avenue Association. 1924.

Page 119: *New York in the Nineteenth Century,* Grafton.